The Original Sentiment

70 INSPIRING LOVE LETTERS

JOSEPH O'RALE

Order this book online at www.trafford.com
or email orders@trafford.com

Most Trafford titles are also available at major online book retailers.

Printed in the United States of America.

ISBN: 978-1-4269-5645-4 (sc)
ISBN: 978-1-4269-5646-1 (e)

Trafford rev. 10/23/2012

www.trafford.com

North America & international
toll-free: 1 888 232 4444 (USA & Canada)
phone: 250 383 6864 • fax: 812 355 4082

Dedication

My heartfelt thanks go first to God for his enabling strength and inspiration that made it possible for this work to be in print.

More grease to my team at **Pilot One Concepts** - You guys are sent from heaven.

Thanks to all my friends and colleagues who were instrumental to the events and opportunities that led to most of the work in this book, one love to you all.

Contents

CELESTIAL INTERCESSION

MAGNETIC MEMOIRS

SEDUCTIVE CEREMONIES

ROMANTIC OUTCRIES

HUMANITY ECHOES

ABSTRACT MATTERS

ILLUSIVE REALITIES

THE GREATEST EXTRA

Introduction

It is absolutely correct the saying that the entire world revolves round the four letter word-LOVE.

The problem bedeviling our world today is based on the lack of this seemingly intangible but most important quality. A family or society where love exists in its entirety is one that enjoys true prosperity, security and continuity of values. And love is the absent ingredient in a society full of insecurity, poverty and other vices.

Joseph O'rale in his 70-chapter notes christened The Original Sentiment; he x-rays all a reader would want to learn about love. His style is unique and a rare depth of thoughts must transport the reader into a world of reality which insincere souls would visit reluctantly. But one thing is sure on getting there. It is a captivating world a departure from which one cannot pretend not to have learnt the basics of life.

Of course today, many often shy away from what reality truly is and this is the result of a world of turmoil. A sincere heart knows when he goes outside the guidelines of love, for only a thin line demarcates the world of love from that of hate.

Lessons learnt from this unique work cannot be recovered from in a hurry, it is highly recommended to patronize what nourishes the soul than that which erodes it of its qualities. In this work lies the truth needed to survive in relationship and life as a whole. Its contents are reader friendly and explanatory enough to instruct and guide in a world where falsehood is fast becoming accepted and where things we used to hold as the truth are now being contested.

Congratulations for having this work in your hands. It is never by accident but by divine order. Please heed this warning however: it would change your thought pattern...but to the positive!

CHAPTER ONE

THE TOAST

The silky honey of my inexhaustible comb
I will proselytize you into before I see my tomb.
Give me a chance to be feathers of your wings,
I am melody; let us soar together as I attach strings.

Call me an exaggeration, label me poppycock.
However, let time reveal the rubies of my stock.
In my desert you brought out the rose in me,
Now my heart is fresh as fish in the sea.

Every breath sketches you a clearer picture;
The sight I confronts is beauty with culture.
Like wax I melt from light into fervent night
My underfoot get slippery, l lose my might.

Be flattered with my extravagance I permit,
Let the shatters unveil our passion betwixt.
As first undefiled appearance of Adam and Eve,
Inseparable with no hidden secret to conceive.

To a union that betters us when comes worst,
To a bond that is glass when we need trust.
I will drink from your love's cup until ghost,
From my cores sincerely, I propose this toast.

I'll proselytize you - Some people are naturally endowed with word power, they easily have their way with just speaking the right words. This is one of the greatest gifts in its raw state to transform any mind. Just as the honey is medicinal, so are the right sweet words, they have the ability to fully convert even the most broken heart to a place of total happiness.

In any relationship where there is a constant break in communication, there is bound to be a loss in affection. Keeping relationship afloat requires the conscious effort of the people involved. Ninety percent of women yearn for assurance in their relationships, they want to be constantly given attention, and they want to truly know that they are the only silky honey in their man's inexhaustible honeycomb.

Women that have experienced one or more heartbreaks tend to resist or rather do not easily succumb to the beauty of words; most of them see men as another predator after its prey. In this, they should be sensitive also not to miss out on a true opportunity.

The rubies of my stock - There is no one who cannot express love. In our individual capacities, we all have a measure of the expression of love and in several ways gifted to express it. Love is as precious as ruby, which also has the color of love; the deep red color is chosen as the universal symbol. Rubies are scarce but when you find them, you have a treasure in your hands so is true about unconditional love when it comes your way.

We all have love stocked in our hearts no matter how much people have hurt us and no matter how many times life has shown us its backside. True love will express itself repeatedly no matter how hurt you are, it always makes your heart as fresh as a fish in the sea, it knows how to mend the broken pieces and use them to build a new foundation in the heart.

Like wax I melt - The passion for a particular thing is what prompts you to give all you have. If you are truly attracted by a vocation or a vision, you can melt for it. It become your number one mission, nothing else seems to be more important than it is. The impetus to do other things becomes irrelevant; your entire energy is redirected and converted to make that particular focus productive. This is what actually makes a mission work and worthwhile.

When the candle exhaust all its light, one thing still remain as its residue and that is the same old wax, though in another form. Our passion and commitment to our relationship and work should be like wax, it should have its bases on truth so that after all the attraction is gone and the purpose is completed, love will still stand out in other refreshed forms.

Undefiled appearance of Adam and Eve - The ability to come out plain and open in every commitment is what generates a strong bond. The reason why some relationship fails is that one or both parties chose to still keep skeletons in their cupboards. People hide certain things about themselves because they feel it would expose their weaknesses if shared. Every page of your life turned remains turned, there's nothing we can really do to reverse it; your faults should be shared as a lesson or an experience to our partners to learn from
If you want your pact to last, you and partner should lay on the table what you want from the relationship and it should be clearly defined what you want the final achievement to look like. In this way, you both work towards a common goal.

I propose this toast - Many people devalue the purpose of a toast, they tend to see it like a mere obeisance. A toast is as much of an expression of faith and love as a seal of appreciation. It has an emotional way of declaring heart felt feelings for the bodies concerned. It has the special purpose of exposing the number one feeling we have towards one another and it goes a long way to tie the knot of friendship and relationship.

CHAPTER TWO

MY HEART'S PRINCESS

Well pleased I am in my beloved princess,
How God has created her to a perfect success.
Her presence makes my tender heart bubble
Every time my majestic world threatens to crumble.
She sits supreme at the golden seat of my mine
Wheeling the affairs of my entity to sublime.
Hidden rays emitted from her made me react,
They filled the vacuum in my princely heart.

My heart is a chest; she is the priceless treasure,
Every time I open up, her twinkles spread pleasure.
Days and nights are packaged to interchange
Nevertheless, her luxury I feel will never age.
With warm embrace, she captured my soul's ship,
Pains and worries erased, on her my love did clip.
She charges the arteries of my routes entirely,
Her love is as a waterfall flowing ceaselessly.

Created her to a perfect success - Beauty they say is in the eyes of the beholder, what would be sugar in your tongue could be salt in another's. We are created individually in our own uniqueness and we appreciate nature in different ways, so sometimes what we call perfect success is obviously rooted more in fantasy than reality. The human faculty concludes quickly by the sight of physical attributes especially when they come in attractive packages.

Perfect success should be classified based not only the physical attribute but also the inward expression. Are the morals of the person in question worthy of emulation? Does he or she satisfy most of the virtues that qualifies a person as charitable? When success is to be measured, the impact it has made on lives must be considered. 'Perfection is unending, so perfect success is progressive'. It extends in a chain process affecting anyone it comes across positively. Therefore, physique is just a part of it, a minor part that attracts but the eye.

She sits supreme - The admiration that easily fades away is infatuation. This could occur when we visualize the person we are involved with as being the perfect lover. When we conclude that the person possesses all the attributes desired in a partner. In reality, no such thing as a 'perfect lover' exists, you just found someone that you are blinded to their flaws. People inspire people with no strings attached so don't be surprised if someone you think you can die for does not return your love.

Check what you are experiencing if it can stand the test of time before going ahead because what looks like love could be a crush or even lust which is short-lived. Everybody get infatuated, it is not wrong but what you do with it determines what it would do to your emotions. One way to get over it is by channeling the time spent in that direction on things that brings out the best in you, engaging in social activities that keep you busy and happy.

Packaged to interchange - The only thing permanent in life is change; everything in nature was made to change. From young to old, from rags to riches, from grass to grace, the changes are countless. The only thing that cannot change is divine love because the very existence of humanity depends on it. There is a luxurious feeling this love can bring to you even if your present state is abject penury. It keeps your dreams alive and constantly assures you there is hope of a better tomorrow. It assures you that your living in pain right now is a training process preparing you to handle the coming gain.

Interchange relates to the concept of giving and receiving. Give love and receive joy. In giving, your hand opens up to receive. One of the decisive tests to prove that you are walking in divine love, that is true love, is giving your time, attention, responsibility and money. Just like the times and seasons, days and nights, every man is packaged to interchange, no one is truly a hard nut.

The arteries of my routes - Some people are born to inspire others. Most people only get inspired by the opposite sex but no matter where it comes from, it should move you in the right direction. The inspiration derived from love is capable of creating a gusto that could cause you to focus tenaciously on your assignment.

The artery represents the most important part of one's routes and it properly channels the inspiration it receives from within and without to give life a proper painting. This inspiration could come from people we admire and cherish including their work or lifestyle. The amazing thing is that one little inspiration could open one up to several other undiscovered talents and the chain could go on and on, never remaining static but changing from one level of flow to another.

CHAPTER THREE

MUCH MORE THAN MOST

Something sweeter than honey,
Much more valuable than money.
Something more celebrated than success,
More in super abound than excess.
Something more like a melodious song,
Flowing from a heavenly tongue.
Something more touching than the opera,
Much more soothing than a whisper.

Something more intoxicating than wine,
More like on a spending spree without a dime.
Something that can hang on a shoestring,
Yet doing the natural super of a door hinge.
Something more like the twinkling of stars,
More ravishing than exotic cars.
Something worth celebrating than the toast,
My feeling for you is much more than most.

Something sweeter than honey - Could there really be anything sweeter than honey? Could there be something truly valuable than money? These questions will have different answers based on our individual differences. If there should be anything sweeter than honey and more valuable than money, then it should render contentment that is encompassed with full gratification. Contentment can make hunger seem like a fresh feeling. It can be likened to a melodious song from a heavenly tongue because it cannot be quantified in material terms; it supersedes more than meets the eye. True love is sweeter than honey and valuable than all the treasure on the earth; it is blind to failure and proves to be the sight to success.

Soothing than a whisper - In a world where love in its different facets become the basis of every long - lasting union, you cannot but embrace it in any form it chooses to surface. If it decides to come in the wind of whispers then it could connote intimacy, an evidence of affection or an existence of an attraction from a body to the other involved. In this condition, your breath plays a greater role rather than the sound of your voice when expressing what you mean.

A whisper goes a long way to expressing the seriousness of an expression. It goes miles to express the efficacy or an emphasis in a speech or dialogue. The tone with which you relay a message is as important as the message itself. We could send the right message but if the tone is wrong, the message would make no meaning. A whisper is a powerful soothing tool because it can calm down a troubled mind. It works like pouring chilled water on a boiling mind.

More intoxicating than wine - The intoxication of wine has the effect of making one live in a dream world where no sorrows and pains exist. It has the temporary ability of keeping one in an excited state despite crucial and turbulent times. True excitement that is generated from the soul within has a most permanent effect. An excited mind is a turbine of ideas; it generates and regenerates ideas endlessly. The after effect of the intoxication of wine is adverse, its after effect renders the mind dull and inactivate but the one generated from the innards is highly productive.

The Natural Super of a Door Hinge - No matter how heavy a door seems to be, little hinges are responsible for swinging it. No matter how large a problem poses to you, it can be solved by a little brilliant idea. No matter how hard a nut is, there is always a soft spot by the corner where you can gradually break into it. A matchstick is little but a little spark from its scratch on a city soaked with gas and the rest is history.

These instances are the mighty acts of little things. We should always tend the little things. Little drops of water can make a mighty ocean and when it becomes mighty, no matter how much water you fetch from them, it never shows. Great businesses and corporations started small. Starting small gives you the advantage of learning how to handle risk to the minimal.

Much more than most - Most times, our feeling find no vocabulary or mere words to express themselves. The feelings a man possess for his loved one cannot be fully emphasized and explained, this always make the act of love look foolish. You cannot clearly explicate on the source of joy that springs from a happy union. When extremists fall in love, nothing else matter; they are willing to die a thousand times for the love to keep existing.

CHAPTER FOUR

VOLCANIC ERUPTIONS

Here was I, high and lying on my magma,
Drained at the floors of love's ladder.
Then you came, the fragrance of a red rose,
Your sweet smell made my interests arouse.
Now I wear smiles and can once again bite,
As I hold you into thousands of night.

My world spun from gloom to bloom,
Spectrum colors were all over my loom.
I wove with the eagerness of a beaver,
A junkie I'm turned, addicted to my lover;
Sniffing and sipping,
Her scent that chokes my surrounding.
I rejoice even as the feeling is complex
And it drags me from my stones to the apex.

Hand in hand, you took me down the aisle,
With joy and the happiness we couldn't deny.
Where our companionship was sealed forever
And our love was laid on the altar.
Here I am, erupting this unending flow
From a heated heart, my sensitive volcano.

Laying on my magma - This statement looks contradictory, lying in a low level and at the same time high. Some people allow circumstances to control their thoughts and all other efforts in their lives when actually there's no circumstance beyond their control. You could be lying in a melted condition where your whole world seems to have crumbled and still maintain a self-confidence that things could only get better.

Don't keep to yourselves in soberness because you haven't seen what you deeply desire as you become vulnerable to a complex attitude. No matter how superior you claim to be, your weakness will surface when you fall in love for the right reasons.

A red rose - This is a symbol of true love. This love makes a sorrowed life blossom with happiness. The fragrance of a red rose is symbolic to the feeling of youthfulness when perceived with an open heart, regardless of age and time. It makes you feel life is an unending dream into thousands of night, as if you would never wake up to reality. It never allows the suspicion that you could ever hurt again.

Addicted to my lover - Love is the most powerful force on planet earth. One minute you are gloomy and another minute love radiates sunshine on your face. It has a captivity-turning force that always leaves you dumbfounded like a dreamer, you begin to see the world as a colorful place to live in and no matter what hurt or wrong people have done against you, you are bound to see humor in it all; everything just seem to reflect sweetness.

A junkie I'm turned - If you are caught up with the addiction of love, you won't mind spending your last cent. You will begin to see the most complex situations as simple, just the way a junkie want to get to the apex of being high without caring to count the cost. In a relationship where true love exists, partners are ready to sacrifice and willing to share all. This is the inevitable power of love

Down the aisle - The aisle is the passage between the members of your sect where they could see you in exhibition of your professed love, commitment and the nature of your true self. A relationship where the people involved are ashamed to come out openly at a time, one where they cannot move hand in hand, has something other than love existing between them - lust, pity or may be one of them is a leech. The foundation of such relationship is insecure and insincere. True love knows no shame, sees no blame and accepts all that looks lame. The place where mere friendship steps into a committed relationship is the beginning of true love.

My sensitive volcano - The force of love is capable of tearing down walls of pain to allow the passage of gain. Most of the mountains we see in our mind's eye will never become reality; they will just be mere troubling thoughts. The continuous expressions of love are like the waterfalls that never end, and it can affect every aspect of our lives. It has a way to stream into the way we move, speak and even what we wear. A heated heart is a heart bubbling for expression, it is always ready to render to people in need, always ready to share a little kindness, and it is as a sensitive volcano ready to erupt at the slightest stimulation.

CHAPTER FIVE

SWEET TALK

Coated with the velvet of pomposity
And spitting with the swagger of a celebrity.
She drifts to the corner where I had my seat,
Her breath smelt nothing short of deceit
And words flowing like a coat of many colors,
They spun a yarn worth millions of dollars.

All I heard were melodies similar to old school rhymes
But they just seem to come from long distant miles.
So spiced were the echoes from her lips,
A mighty ocean could form from her sweet drips.
I was blown away with captivating winds,
Losing my caution, my culture and my grids.

One moment we were in the Garden of Eden,
Another and my suspicion began its bidding.
Quickly I subdued my hypnotized element
And withdrew from the shell of her worded regiment.
I bounced back with my armour to ward off her toxin
And developed fast fins as I swam far from her regime.

Coated with the velvet of pomposity: Many of us do not actually plan to exhibit pride when we meet others. What we miss out is to be able to display effectively the rule of first impression. When we meet people for the first time, we should learn to be moderate in our expression otherwise we could end up being termed as liars. If your first impression is filled with lies, you have to build on that with the same bricks and what a great fall that awaits your personality on the day your secret is uncovered.

All I heard were melodies: When you meet some people the first time, their conversation seem so good to be true. They run you a perfect education, perfect relationship and perfect dream. It's already become a law not to talk of the rigours that made that relationship perfect or rather kept it in line with perfection. Nothing on earth is truly without pain, if you want to experience gain then get ready to run the race of pain. Melodies, sweet songs, beautiful sound came up out of hours of practice, re-practice and improvement.

So spiced were the echoes: If you have a way with words and you were born to talk, then you can reach the top faster than anybody else. If you can express your feelings effectively when interacting and even marketing, the sky is your beginning. Everyone would listen to anything you have to say when you can hold them spellbound in your conversation. The same goes for any relationship because communication is key. If you must keep the doors of happiness open constantly, you must apply this key.

Losing my caution: Throwing away caution is a conscious act and it's within your powers to hold on; but losing your caution is not deliberate you just can't help it. You gradually lose it without even realizing it until it hits you on the face. No matter how much our principles are firm, love can dissolve it. Christians drop all their former culture and adopt the life of Christ likewise every other religion. Love for any pursuit will always drain you of former passions and before you know it, you can tell a great difference from where you were and where you are.

And fast fins to swim: Stay clear off anything that wouldn't add value to your personality and your plans, whether persons, ideas or counsel. The time spent talking about events and people is best spent remodeling and improvising old ideas or better still building new ideals. It is better you turn back immediately you realize you are on the wrong track than to look for ways to amend and compromise on your plans. Be sensitive to discern sweet talk and love at first sight, it will save you the troubles of a lot of things.

CHAPTER SIX

WITH YOU

When you are present,
Sweetness hovers around my tent;
Keeping me extremely warm
From whatever pain and storm.

When you speak,
Meekness covers the words you pick;
Leaving me rest assured
That our hearts are in one accord.

When I listen to you,
Gentleness takes over my cue;
Painting my heart with cares
Something I only envisaged for years.

Sweetness hovers: When you are around people and things that inspire you, there is a great tendency to achieve a lot from the inspiration. When two people are deeply in love and they care for each other, there erupts a brilliant result. Love has its way and no one can explain it fully, it can make a troubled man forget all his demise. The feeling of a loved one close to you brings the kind of warmth that comes with security.

When you speak: Word has the most powerful creative effect on the planet. If you want to shut all the doors of opportunity in your life, shut your mouth. Words are the waters of your dream plants, after conceiving a dream, you need to continually speak about them and as you do, you are releasing the most important support for your dream plant to mature rapidly. Our choice of word matters a lot. Negative words end up having sad effects upon our lives and positive words will leave us full of happiness. The words you speak can instantly determine the general state of your heart.

When I listen to you: The words we listen to are like seeds. If we accept them, they find a place in our heart to settle and grow. If we do not, they are discarded just as they came. If you conceive the wrong statements in your heart, you have not only polluted your heart but your entire system. It will not take long before you begin to show its fruits in your character. Be choosy about what you hear and discard what won't be of benefit to your spiritual growth instantly.

Gentleness takes over: Greatness will reflect from your life when you fashion your heart to instantly repel what is not in line with your principles. You can build yourself to a place where you don't need to struggle to choose what will not gratify your soul. If you keep the right people around you at all times, you will hear the right words and your life will be defined. This goes also to the kind of movies you watch, the kind of clubs and association you join. If any activity in them repels your spirit, drop them immediately.

Painting my heart: Everyone loves attention. We all cherish being the centre of attraction if not fully it. Attention makes us feel wanted; it can double up the speed of our inspiration. When you make someone know you truly care for them, you make them more committed to you. If they do not show true commitment then they are afraid of letting you down, they are not really ready to stay with you.

CHAPTER SEVEN

LONGING

The thoughts of you get me excited on and on,
Inside me bubbles like a national lottery won.
I still remember the first time you met me,
You wanted to say a million words instantly.

I still feel the force of your speech,
You were so hungry to have me within reach.
We made plans for "what happens here stays here";
How we'll hold hands and walk up the streets there.

Such sweet feeling was exuded from you,
And a perfect scenario you painted before my view.
This emotion you set in me keeps burning
Long even after you left without a goodbye or warning.

The thoughts: Thinking is part of the living process, if you don't think you won't improve. Every good and bad thing that was created came out of thoughts. Do not pity your brain, work it and it will eventually give you a definite way to come out of your challenges. Pleasant thoughts are necessary in the life of every individual to spread as the base for inspirations that bring happiness and truth. Only genuine inspirations will get you excited on and on every time you meditate on them.

I still remember: To reminisce is to check where you are coming from in comparison to where you are and it is necessary if you want to get to where you are going. The memorable things of our past and what more is expected of us are one of greatest forces to propel us to our desired future. If you want to know what you should be up to, reminisce on your past encounters in relation to your present, you will get a clear pointer to where you should be and what you should be doing. Nobody should believe in your future like you do.

And made plans: 'What happen here stays here' is the slogan of Las Vegas. It is characterized as one of the world's most popular gambling resort and a beautiful sight to visit. Love can play a similar role, it could be so real and beautiful, and before you know it all, your emotions have been gambled away. Most times true love don't come in attractive packages, you keep it closely for sometime and weigh it critically to determine where it's coming from and heading to.

And a perfect scenario: When a man wants to get a woman to love and cherish him, he should paint a perfect view of his future and where he wants their relationship to end. This is to assure the woman of his intentions if they are truly genuine. No relationship can attain a perfect scenario for the ups and downs, the quarrels and settlements are the bricks that build up the relationship. If a woman wants to play the same role, she might end up wasting her time because it won't be long before a man wants to find someone he can really express his feeling to, he would want an opportunity to display his manhood essence.

Long even after you left: Feelings that really imparts can last long after their contact. They could be either positive or negative and they create an indelible impression in our heart. This is the same principle first impression is based on, the first one lasts so long that the second impression does not always have a chance. Anytime you are opportune to present an impression especially when it's the first one, give it well and create a lasting aura of who you are and can be.

CHAPTER EIGHT

INTOXICATION

One more thought of you is like another glass of wine,
You keep eating up my heart and making my soul sublime.
My mind is saturated with pages of you and me,
I cannot erase the pictures to make me see clearly.
My vision is blurred and I see everything in twos
But it's both of us in view when I seriously deduce.

I floated in the clouds,
Broke all standing bounds.
More wine and more wine
And your face filled every space and line.
Forth and back I swayed,
Like the pines on a windy day delayed.
I was so drunk with your love to stupor
But I felt so good in the misdemeanor.

You keep eating up my heart: Love is a dangerous game. If you can, by all means keep your eyes open when playing it. So many have been killed by it and many more have been healed by it. Its divine nature has made it a tool in the hands of the faithful and even the infidel. The only love that will prove its worth is one that has its foundation laced with selflessness because many have chosen to give love because they receive same. If you will allow your heart to be consumed, let it be by the kind of love that seeks no interest in return.

But it's just only us in view: When you truly love someone, your mind is full of him/her. You wake up and wonder what they are doing, whether they have eaten and most times everything seems to centre on them. Many just profess love but have never really fallen in it. If you don't feel him/her like a second skin then check your feelings. It is more than you are so occupied with your career that's why you don't think of them. Love has time. It creates its own corner, its own space, and its own view.

I floated in the clouds: When you are in love, you tend to lose most of your personal decisions. It is no longer just you but you and your partner. The climax of a relationship entails that two shall become one. When you are alone, you could take fixed decision and keep your ideologies permanent but when there is another person or person(s) involved you need to float your ideas to the board and be ready to come to a compromise when there is need to merge the collective decisions. The rules always have to be flexible when there are other people with you, otherwise, you will be termed a dictator.

Like the pines on a windy day: Windy here symbolizes the action of speaking for longer than necessary and in a way that is not easily interpreted and understandable. Love sometimes exhibits this attribute. You just find out that all effort to interpret it becomes more complicated. Pines are evergreen, they keep the leaves fresh all through the year, and this is love itself for its fire never really dies. It can automatically turn fresh anytime you want it to be. It sways in any direction the wind blows it to, very obedient, very loyal, always waiting for you to take that bold step so it could move after you.

But I felt so good in the misdemeanor: The only good thing about misdemeanor is that it becomes an example to others. If you listen to the tales of people who have suffered heartbreaks and why it happened, you could avoid such in your relationship. Most of them will tell you when they were in blind love, they know something could be wrong but they just couldn't help it. You must learn to guard your heart and define the basis of your affection at every stage of your association.

CHAPTER NINE

FROM A THOUSAND MILES

As I shut my eyes, you and I started to travel,
We held our hands and walked as a couple.
It was a union neither of us planned to start,
Now it chimes continuously like a cataract.
You are far away yet so close to my fences
And I'm losing my resolve, my fist and tenses.

A thousand miles is drawn near with my eyes shut,
You came so close and leaned on my fort.
I'm falling into the cobs of your web
As your sweet speeches settle in my head.
It takes me through the barriers of our distance
And brings your embrace to my chest in an instance.

As I shut my eyes: Meditation is one of the ways the mind receives divine inspiration. If you see a man that doesn't take time out of his busy schedule to meditate, you have seen a man who is most likely not to appreciate the essence of life. Witty inventions are the products of meditation and action. When you mediate you are placed on the road of acceleration. When you shut your eyes to things of the world, you open your eyes to things that are not physical. Create a time everyday to engage the act of meditation and see appreciation evolve from your life.

You are far away: There is no distance in the spirit realm. Everything a man desires is within his reach. Before God sent His son to die for humanity, man communicated with Him via mediums and prophets. Today He has released his love and broken every barrier before man, He communicates with him directly. We all have equal opportunity to access His throne of mercy. The death and resurrection of Jesus broke the distance between the physical and the spiritual realm.

A thousand miles: Nothing is as distant as it seems if you are willing to over look the process of time. Any distant love affairs can survive if there is constant communication; it renews the mind constantly on the expectations of the relationship. 'Most people can communicate better when they are distant and express their innermost heart desire than when they see their loved ones face to face'. Love knows no distance; it only understands the language of communication and expression.

As your sweet speeches: When you continue to listen to and believe in the words you hear, they will definitely have an impact upon your life. People are swindled because they believed the lies bestowed on them, there's nothing that is absolutely free and there's no short cut to getting wealth or being established in love. Every speech prepared in deep meditation has its power of influence; it has the potentiality to cause the change it is meant for. The effect of a speech becomes heavier when the ones delivering it have a brand name attached to their identity.

Taking me places: Love has its own route; it's quite different from where one normally plans to follow. Love can cancel the routine of your everyday schedule and keep you in a place just synchronizing with the one you love. It can build and as well destroy the principles that guard your lifestyle. It shouldn't be toyed with by teens but practiced by the mature minds who can handle it. Do not accept and digest any sweet speech you hear, this game of love is a highly delicate one to play. The only love to be trusted in full measure is the one from above, the divine love of God.

CHAPTER TEN

A LOVE LETTER TO MARY

Dear Mary, I know life fetches you the best from its well
For the glow in your eyes always sounds a joyful bell.
Deny astonishment when this package of words you behold,
They are wonderful fresh words that have never been sold.
From my windows I saw the radiance in your reflection
And bred suggestions that I give our friendship an extension.
The sugar in my tea and the only goldfish in my sea,
Mere words fail in expression of your true meaning to me.
Your golden voice reaches my heart and clicks like a jackpot,
Drilling holes straight to my marrow and inducing comfort.

Mary my love, my feeling plays like a favourite song;
Soul - inspiring, heart - stirring, they couldn't be wrong.
There crescents a rainbow across the surface of my cloud,
Let glide to hold it and make our love renowned.
I make a vow to dare and care for you, bear and share with you;
I'm willing to spare that love that leaves all men without a clue.
Please welcome me to your world as I knock on the door,
Give me the chance to show you the treasure I have in store.
If you shut me out, to debacle I might lose myself;
My arms open in wait for your warmth; it's me, Joseph.

Dear Mary: We place value on only the people and things that are dear to us and at the top of our priorities. These turn out to be the group that inspires us as we forge ahead to our desired goal. When someone is dear to you, you cannot wish him bad or think evil of that person. People who are not dear to us seemingly waste our time and bore us when they come around. It is best to be around the ones that are dear to our heart for they have the tendency to make us feel celebrated.

They are wonderful fresh words: When you are genuinely inspired, the words that come out of you will definitely surprise you. You can copy and use words that have been in existence but the words generated by a genuine inspiration or touch are fresh and incomparable. Love can make you manufacture the kind of words that leaves you dazed, it can make you create your own vocabularies and a style of operation that has never been used. Nothing of all these will come when there is no object of affection which serves as the vehicle for fresh words.

Drilling straight to my marrows: The induction of true love can make you experience the touch of a lifetime. Very few things can touch us deeply. There are extreme greed, strong jealousy, the crave for excessive wealth and these are in the line of wrong virtues.
The strong desire to accomplish a goal, to satisfy a loved one and keep her or him happy and the eminent pursuit to see the realization of the kingdom of God are virtues on the right side that will see us go far in life.

I'm Willing: Willingness is a gift that is bestowed on us instantly at the inception of affection. You don't need to be persuaded to be willing; it is backed up by a free flowing effort when your zeal is in the right form. You are automatically charged to go all the way being willing to serve, to be served and to achieve the goal attached to your zeal. Anything you are ready to give your all to will end up bringing all to you. The reason we achieve our dreams and visions will not be complete without attributing a measure of recognition to this virtue.

Give me the chance: We all need a chance if we must discover our potentialities and composition. Chance is the opportunity that our preparedness encounters to bring our breakthrough to reality. You never know when your time is actually coming if you don't move and take the chance before you. Whether the chance becomes successful or not, you should go after it because it could just be that one chance your gift is actually waiting for to find full expression, it could just be that one that will present you to the right person needing your service.

CHAPTER ELEVEN

LOVE CHORUS

I thought I'd never see love again,
With a conclusion that all of them were the same.
Until I was caught up in your perfume
And my pains and pressures you did consume.
You were like the rains sent in drought
To shower a new love all over my tender heart.
If I sleep in death this very moment
My life would be an eternal complement.

Come what may, you'll ever be my diamond,
You made me realize the meaning of a bond.
If I were to make an exchange for you,
The world would be worthless to the wine you brew.
Every time of my life with you is a lifetime,
You gave my sound meaning with prestigious chime.
I'll forever cherish your entrance into my ship
For sailing with me and touching me so deep.

I thought I'd never: Never conclude on any situation, change is a miracle that can take place in a split second. There is no success with an end; the day it ends is the day its failure is born. Love knows no bound, chooses no specific territory or any style it wishes to express itself. It will never announce its arrival, it is when you least expect that it comes to shock you by consuming your heart. Everyone loves in different ways and expresses their heart felt feelings differently, so be ready for its unexpected expression.

Until I was caught up: When your pain is over, you cannot really tell the extent of the pressures because the consummation joy brings to the heart will give no place to such. We need to get caught up in something for our lives to make a meaning. Until we are caught up we can't be eaten up. Getting caught up entails every fibre of your being re-channeling all its energy to one point of reference. If you find yourself caught up and consumed by a vision there is nothing you can really do about it, it will keep you restless till you achieve it.

To shower a new love: No matter how dark it is, your love towards someone or something will made life easier. There is always a new love to be experienced with someone new or a new thing. In the journey of love there's always something new at every junction, it depends on you to take the route you want. If you are willing to experience something fresh, then you must be willing to risk out your faith. A new love experience can turn your whole life around and bring out the other side of you. Those that know you deeply and see it will recognize it and tell you.

If I were to make an exchange: A man that can sell and buy his love has not yet found genuine love. No value could be placed on love if it is real. If it's quantifiable then something else is in play. Silver, gold and diamond will give you extreme satisfaction but this will leave you sober in your days. When you amass wealth for the wrong reasons you get burdened with the objection to spending it. God's love for us seeks no interest; He is not after us looking for ways to pay Him so we can live our own lives the way we want. God want us to have the mind of Christ He want us to work with Him as one mind to fulfill the yearning of His kingdom.

My sound has meaning: Life is like a song, if you play it well its melodious sound will attracts others to you. If you play it wrongly you'll end up scaring people from you and lose a lot of goodwill and benefits. Everything about you speaks; your mood, your gesture, your opinion and your philosophy say a lot about you. Let your words be seasoned and filled with meaning so you could be an example to others.

CHAPTER TWELVE

LOVE LINES

Not everyday people fall in love at first sight,
Many of us subdue the good feeling and fight.
If love were a spark of fire, an ocean cannot quench it;
It consumes the hardest soul and will never quit.

True love will keep you from the thin line
As you board the sentimental ship in its prime.
If it's real, it will stand the test of time;
If it's true, our hearts must sublime.

Slowly but surely we shall become one mind
And everything we worked for will be refined.
Let's attain one day at a time and cherish the moments
And enjoy the freedom as glide in its currents.

Not everyday: Love at first sight is a spontaneous affair which nobody plans for when they step daily. People fall in love at first sight because the object of attraction fits the imagination of a stored up dream. Falling in love at first sight is a captivating experience; it fills you with extreme joy and seeming fulfilment. If it stands, then it was meant to be; if it doesn't then infatuation was in play somewhere. This kind of love rarely stands.

If love were a spark: Many water cannot quench love, nothing can extinguish the flame that erupts from it. You can pretend to be strong against its power but all you do is making yourself suffer in silence. If you are one of those people who suppress the feeling out of ego, you are only causing distractions for yourself because no matter how much you try to concentrate, the love you refuse to share will keep resurfacing in your thoughts. No man can resist the allure love brings, it has no respect for your muscles, it don't care how tall you are and what you have been through to become hardened.

If it's real: If love is real, then it doesn't need any back up explanation. If you wait in patience its true colour will evolve. The reason you need true love is because it possesses the capability to retain its power, every other attributes surrounding it stand just to complement. Beauty, brains are complements of love and they can fade and fail. If you love for the sole fact that love is mutual and divine, you'll stand in the day when every other attributes fade away.

Slowly but surely: When your plans are concise and accurate, the term 'failure' becomes obsolete. Its better you spend months planning the success of a feat than rushing to achieve and crashing in a few weeks. Planning to take some short cut will only cut you short along the line. Love should be handled in time and stages if you must see it bloom in full colour. Cherish every second, every minute and hour of it, the more you appreciate it, the more it responds to your thoughts. One small distraction in love could make you see your partner or loved one as an enemy.

And enjoy the freedom: Love can set you free and turn your life around. A little love shown to others becomes like a seed in their heart which germinates and eventually takes over the soul of that person. If you plan to achieve everything in a day without love, you have planned to succeed with bitterness waiting at the tail end. Life is meant to be enjoyed in love for it is one of the sources of sound health and mind.

CHAPTER THIRTEEN

LOVE BOAT

I'm swimming in the pool of her juice,
All her waves are taking me on a jolly cruise.
Here is the place I want to capsize and drown,
For since I met her I never felt a frown.

I'm softly killed everyday as I flow in her sails,
This love overcomes the billows and never derails.
Wherever her rudder turns, there I'll be found,
As we fulfill an eternal trip beyond every bound.

I'm as a seaman and she is the captain;
My movements and instructions are from her to obtain.
She has taken over the sights of my binoculars,
I've lost control; I do everything from behind her bars.

I'm swimming: When it is genuine love you have for someone close to your heart nothing can stop you. Anyone that tries to caution on your deep feelings is making himself your enemy. It's a greater offense if you give them your ears and their advice crosses certain boundaries. Love creates its own opinion and views when it consumes you and other things which does not tally with your discovery become contrary and regarded as an opposition. Love creates its own world in your mind's eye and gives you the opportunity to see the inward beauty of the other person.

Here is the place: Love is definite. It knows exactly where it is headed and will eventually hit its mark. Our emotions need to be tried and tested to determine the kind of love we are experiencing. Any profession of love that has not stood the test of time is built on a foundation which cannot be trusted. If someone says they love you, put them to the test to determine if it's real. If someone truly loves you, they will be willing to let the world know no matter what may happen. Evil is bred in secret, if love is to be hidden then there is something not pure about it. It gives light so it cannot be hidden; when love is shared in secret, it is not meant to be or something is not just right.

This loves overcomes: Every relationship has its dark days and if you are not prepared to stand it, you might be washed away when the storm comes. When the love we share is real, its foundation is sure. The nature of true love is so pure and a lot of people respect it, this has become the basis of deception for people who deceive others in the name of love. We tend to listen to people who present themselves as lovable or when they show seemingly true love towards us.

I'm a seaman: A seaman does whatever his captain orders him to do. He is being paid to run the casual errands and do the menial jobs in a boat or ship. Love can do the same to you; it can make you do things you wouldn't do in normal circumstances and to worsen it, without demanding for any form of settlement. You can sacrifice anything if you are truly trapped in the web of genuine love. That is why we all are vulnerable when it comes to this issue. Love is a sacrificial boat, when you sail in it you have to take precaution because the security of your cruise lies not in your expertise or smartness but on God's divine help.

She has taken over: It is abnormal to be in the total control of someone who does not consider any of your ideals and comments. You could be led in the wrong direction if you find yourself in this fate. Love could be possessive and it should be equally addressed when you notice this trait before it gets out of hand. When love consumes you, you are bound to view all things from your lover's perspective and not from yours; you would prefer to take decision with the way your lover thinks.

CHAPTER FOURTEEN

THE WHEELS OF LOVE

Nothing stands before us a hurdle un-crossable;
The world is one village in our palms feasible.
We choose the tunnel of hatred in our sojourns,
Destined to take all the bulls by their horns.

We wheel towards every earth's reproach
And shine on them hope like the Olympic torch.
Medals fall on the plains we chart
And greatness embellishes our craft.

Wherever our wheels ride upon
Changes are wrought in excess return.
On the roads of competition we throttle
To make loving easier and simple.

Nothing stands before us: There is nothing new that hasn't happened before. No problem anyone passes through is entirely strange, the wonderful thing is that time will always make a way of escape. Our problems have a way of becoming extinct, when they have stayed with us longer then necessary. 'Any challenges you can't crossover will eventually pass over'. It is when we overcome challenges that we are regarded as champion and that is when we can determine our strength.

We choose the tunnel: If we must make a name in our lifetime, we must follow the road that has rarely being traveled by men. Greatness comes with problems we solve and the inventions we narrow upon; it doesn't come with the wide and easy road. The world is full of problems and void of men who are ready to take time out to discover the solutions. Everyone is in a rush to satisfy his personal needs and the needs of their immediate families because of inadequacies in the system. Check those that have become a household name, they have done what many were afraid to do. There is no easy and smooth way to greatness.

And shine hope: Let everything you do bring a glimmer of hope to someone. Let your life be a spiritual guide to people, the light which leads them as they search for fulfilment. When the basis of everything you do is love, the light of your life will shine before them. When hope is postponed, the heart of a man can become sick. When the heart is sick, man totally loses his composition and his faith. If it's in your power to render good to others, do not delay.

Changes are wrought: If the essence of your deeds is honest, positive changes are bound to occur. Even If they don't produce the kind of result you want to see, you will at least see a change of heart in you. Whether it's a positive change in what you are doing or in your heart, you'll enjoy the fulfillment. The only factor in life that ever remains indefinite is change, it can never be static. It is either things are changing for good and you are seeing tangible progress or the situation is moving from bad to worse before it finally dies. Before anything dies you have the early opportunity to set it right, it depends on you.

On the roads of competition: Life is a competition. Compete it in. It is not in exceeding the result of others to stand as the one and all but to do all you can to overtake your former success. If you are doing the same thing constantly, you won't get a different result until you devise a different pattern. Life becomes easier if we see positive changes and results in all we do.

CHAPTER FIFTEEN

JOURNEY WITH LOVE

Here lies what is to be of our vision,
The four cardinal points but for one decision.
I'm deeply troubled on which paths to tread,
I need one that would put sweetness on my bed.

Suddenly there came a perfect beam
Followed by the sound of solemn hymn.
It was your voice reading out a guide
And it showed me the path we should abide.

I went after you without looking back,
The journey was blissful for I knew no lack.
Your canopy of love was my hope and shield;
From mischievous tongues our love was sealed.

Ours was a smooth ride free from bumps;
I was glad I danced to the rhythm of our drums.
My heart became the place of enlightenment,
Now all doubts erased I'm dealing on merriment.

The Four cardinal points: In life we have a million and one professionals and none of them is inferior to another because they all have their importance and none can exist without the other. Every profession a man desires has one end; to fulfil ambition, or a vision or to cater for his family. The pointer of vocations has so many tentacles but with one goal and that is fulfilment in whatever form it comes. Whatever point you choose to pin your desires on and you keep at it will definitely get you to your destination.

Suddenly there came: Divine ideas come when you least expects them. Such an idea will never put you under intense pressure to bring it to actualization. If an idea is divine, whatever it needs to get it accomplished will also come your way. If you can keep your mind in sincere focus as you did when you got the idea, the provision for it will emerge. God will not implant an idea in you the one you cannot accomplish, if you are capable of doing it, He impresses it in your heart and directs you to people for support who will assist you to bring it to pass.

I went after you: You might live the rest of your life wishing you have gone after a particular decision if you don't take it. It is better you fail in it and have total peace knowing where you made mistakes than living in the regret of not making a move. If you set your heart to serve God, do not look back. The fact that you took that step means you believe in His promises. It is easier to forget all His promises when you are distracted or when you choose to be. Go after God with all you've got and you'll end up having a good report.

Your canopy of love: Love covers all flaws and faults, which is why when someone is truly in love he becomes deaf to pieces of advice and pleas to what and the way things really are. You cannot really come between what two people in love are sharing most times because you could clearly see they are consumed in their attributes, attitude and style. The strength of love shelters all and nobody under it can give you an explanation you can comprehend. People may say all kinds of things and call you all sorts of name to bring a separation but it just keeps your love going stronger.

Now all doubts erased: Divine love from above is the only one that can erase all uncertainty of life. The love between humans will always have doubts hovering above it because of the fragility of our beings. We all are prone to suddenly become what we didn't bargain for overnight. The presence of doubt is the absence of faith. Love doesn't work that way especially the love of God, it ignores doubts. You must be fully inclined to Him for you to enjoy the benefits.

CHAPTER SIXTEEN

THE WISDOM OF LOVE

Up above He sat on a great white throne.
By the Father's right side who gave Him all to control.
Down below was sin and grief luring the hearts of men
'Son, go and redeem my people from this den';
He said, 'Restore the lame and give them their desired fame.
And humble as a lamb He stepped down the ladder of affluence
To loose the locks that held humanity from her essence.
He took the stripes to ensure our sound health
And procured our safety when he defeated death.
Evil would have done all to keep Him alive
If it knew His resurrection would spring thousands of life.
What love dwells in our source of existence;
Revealing His wisdom to give us true influence.

Up above He sat: The manifestation of God the Father as the Omniscient is such that He knows the thoughts and intents of everyone in the world. He knows whatever you are passing through. Nothing transpires in the world without His knowledge. God manifests in various ways; as the Omnipresent, He is present everywhere at the same time. God is never more than a second away. He also manifests as the Omnipotent, the one having total power that is able to do anything. He is the master of the universe.

Down below was sin and grief: The world will actual become what you want it to be for you. You have the ability to create your world. If you see the world as a place of sin and grief, then it's time to begin a change which must start with yourself. Jesus Christ came that sin and grief may give way to peace and joy. The devil is all out to make the people of God never experience their full potential but God has sent His son, Jesus Christ to help man fulfill his true purpose on earth. You can decide to abstain and refrain from things of the world and live a purposeful life.

He took the stripes: Before the death of Jesus, He was made to undergo scourging, pierces and bruises. This He did for Humanity so we could start a new life in God, a life free from sin, sickness and sorrow. Every time we see the cross and acknowledge what Christ did for us, His love fills our heart and manifests his glory. Scholars say there are thirty nine (39) deadly diseases in the world and it was recorded that the Lord Jesus during the crucifixion received thirty-nine (39) stripes on our behalf. It apparently means Jesus took all the deadly diseases in His death and His resurrection has brought us new life.

Evil would have done all: If the forces of evil existing in the world knew that crucifying Jesus would spring up millions of His likes, they would have done all to protect His life. The wisdom of God looks foolish to men every time because we can never fully comprehend the ways of God. If He allows evil to prevail at a point then it must be for a greater weight of glory in the latter end.

Revealing His wisdom: Today God has made His wisdom so express more than in the ages past. You can never fathom some of the new inventions that spring up every time, it can only be from a source greater than the intelligence of man. If Jesus had not come to die, man wouldn't have the opportunity to access the Spirit of God. It is this same spirit that works in man to divinely inspire him to all his invention. The revelation of God's wisdom to man has made him wiser than evil force that rules the world. You must connect with Him to be able to defeat the wiles of the world.

CHAPTER SEVENTEEN

THE FIGHT FOR LOVE AND FREEDOM

I suddenly realized I have been caged on a seat,
And fetters were as bangles on my hands and feet.
I thought I was living in absolute freedom,
Not knowing I was tagged from where I came from.

I shook vehemently to make the shackles divide,
And down they came with the walls on every side.
I was free again to fly but I barely had wings,
Life became a sweet sensation as I dangle on its swings.

Every new step was supposed to be free and fair,
Still I struggle to conquer all that laces me with jeer.
This love I now steered is worth fighting for,
My troubled conscience has received an everlasting cure.

And fetters were as bangles: You can put yourself in bondage if you do not live with a pure conscience. When you harbour malice, bitterness and strive in your heart you have bound yourself not to experience the transformation love brings. Some people will tell you it is their nature to be malicious and unforgiving, These people can go any length to get back at you in the name of the wrong doings you mistakenly committed against them. This is a false belief on their part for nothing evil can be part of the nature of a man which was not attracted to his life.

I shook vehemently: You can choose to reject anything you don't like in your life. God has given man a free will to do whatever he wants but what will give you fulfillment is walking in His will and ways. The violent in spirit can pull the force of anything they desire their way. "You can pressurize God to give you what you are not due for but it will be premature in your hands and might destroy your destiny". If you receive His gifts at the appropriate times, it makes things easier and you can never be distracted. Sustaining your freedom requires depending on His wisdom.

Life became a sweet sensation: The right to be free is for everyone, no man has the right to hold anyone bound beyond his will. You must learn to grow in freedom so you can have a firm foundation in it. Anyone enjoying love and peace has paid or is paying a price for it. Making life a sweet sensation is a calculated effort, life will be in motion for you when you are practically excite about it. You must place a demand on what you want out of life before you can receive from its abundant supplies.

Everyone new step: After you have fought to retain your right to live in love, you are to work out every new step you take in the consciousness of your integrity and choice. This role sustains you in taking the right step because one wrong step forward could set up many more backward. If you are taking the right steps and you are faced with persecution, do not relent in your pressings for it will bring you into a larger space of freedom. Freedom is in phases, the more you step up, the greater the magnitude of love that comes to you. The greater the love that comes to you the more the responsibility laid in your hands.

My troubled conscience: God speaks to us through our conscience; it is that place where He makes us feel good or guilty according to our doing. God can restrain us from committing an act He doesn't want us to by pricking our conscience. You shouldn't be weary when your conscience troubles you if you are walking in the light, you should be thankful for that is a pointer to exactly where you should go or what you should do.

CHAPTER EIGHTEEN

YOUR TENDER MERCY.

Every time I fall short from your pedestal,
I search for warm tears to make me crystal;
But to astonish me my wells are found so dry
As if you planted this valley for me to come by.
Though my every step saturates with dust,
Still on your staff will I put my trust.
I look beyond all to the streets of gold
Where my soles will remain impeccable until old.

Saved by your grace, sculptured for the call;
Your tender mercy continually caught my fall.
Silver and gold can't take your seat,
Only in your presence, I experience sweet.
Lord, cause streams of my heart to freely flow
So upon me your express light will shower and show.
Your awesome mercy endures until the end,
You beat my imagination, my faithful friend.

From Your pedestal - Every man is born to rule in his own individual world in which he holds the ace to every challenge that present itself. There are certain doors that will remain shut if you refuse to open them to humanity, they will be kept that way until the divine baton is passed on to someone else. A good look down history will expose to you that every great man or woman was celebrated for one special ability they released from their heart of treasures to affect their generation.
Every man is made to be a potential celebrity but until he looses himself from his myopic sphere, he remains a mediocre. Most of us have diverted from where nature has placed us and become someone else's helper in reaching their desired heights when

we should be actualizing ours. The pleasure you derive in other people's treasure will always be short lived. You are at your best in that particular circle that bring out the best in you; that area you excel without stressing your mental or physical ability, and any time you deviate for something else not related, you fall from the circumference where you have been placed.

Search for warm tears - There are certain decisions we make that end up making us shed humble tears, even the right ones. Regret, remorse, defeat, anxiety are some of the poisons that found a way of being loosed from the heart by the antidote of tears. There is always a relief when you shed your pains out in tears. There are times when you are so filled with burdens of frustration and it seems the whole world is against you, the very minute you set yourself apart to search for warm tears, you find your heart is lifted. 'You weep it out to sweep it out'.
One of the ways to achieve this search is by letting the lyrics of your favorite song touch and stir you deeply. There will be days when it does not seem this easy, it will feel like you are in a set up; even your constant search for tears begins to weary you because you are actually in that situation consciously. Your conscience refuses to prick you even when you know you are guilty. It is the Spirit of counsel and might dealing with you to set your motives right.

The streets of gold - Great folks always have this inner drive that darkness will result in morning; that coal could be reformed to gold. They may stand limited by status or physical attributes, but they refuse to see it. Their steps may look unclean with dust but they still believe that it will work out for good. They always have the focus that anything could happen, that they are co-creators with the Vital Force of creation. Long after such people are gone, their memories are unforgettable and their footprints spread indelibly on the sands of time.

Your tender mercy - Mercy is the highest form of undeserved kindness shown to someone you have power over. It is enjoyed only on the platform of the knowledge of its capabilities. It is the function of this virtue that picks any individual from rags to

the kind of riches they saw in their dreams. It has the ability of looking partial because it makes you wonder why certain things happen to certain people and why they do not to others. It is a divine connector that breaks all human protocol.
Sometimes you wonder how you got out of a seemingly dead situation which predicted your waterloo; it is work of Mercy that did it. It catches you when you thought you had fallen and make you stand with bold shoulders. Take a deep thought and you will realize that the greatest kindness you have enjoyed were sweat less. Such experiences always ended up sweet; all the silver and gold in the world can not amount to these wonderful moments.

The streams of my heart - This relates to the unspeakable joy that envelopes the heart when it experiences showers from the light of mercy. You do not have a dime in your pocket, and no food on your table, but you are filled with the satisfaction of fulfillment. This fulfillment could radiate from the inside to create an atmosphere on the outside that could pave way for inexplicable miracles. The formula for this wonder cannot be derived on a mental note, it is totally a mystery. The awesomeness of mercy cannot seize to be a top amazement in our times. It always goes against all odds to beat your imagination. Mercy from above is like a trophy not labored for and should be embraced as a faithful friend.

CHAPTER NINETEEN

STEADFAST DEWS

Sorrows flow into the tender chambers of my heart
As I meditate on what the cross did on my behalf.
Grief wells up in me overflowing through my eyes,
I'm withdrawn to the perpetual state of the wise.
My understanding sharpens, I see your love
Like drizzling rains from pregnant clouds above.
Your steadfastness is a sumptuous and palatable meal,
It's visual so ordinary, yet much stronger than steel.

Neither my shield nor spear was lifted to contend,
For my rights, you stood valiantly to defend.
My heart's chamber enlarges with rejoicing of oil
For Calvary rendered to me such a great spoil.
Sorrows and grief totally despised my company
The afterglow of joy refuses to desert me.
The world can't use its love without hurts
East or West, my home will be in your courts.

What the cross did - The origin of the Christian faith started from the cross on Mount Calvary where Jesus Christ died displaying a total act of love and sacrifice. There is no greater charity than for a man to lay down his life for another. If you are a true Christian, deep thoughts of God's love will always overwhelm your heart. At such times, sweet sorrow finds the opportunity to flow into your heart. Such sorrow is better than laughter because it withdraws one from the world of fantasies and brings one face to face with the reality of wisdom.

Whenever grief, the extremity of sorrow, engulfs a heart, the only remedy for relieve could be to allow tears to flow from your inside through the eyes. This is a perfect time for deep meditation because it places you in a solemn mood.

Sumptuous and Palatable meal - A meal may be small but if impressive and pleasant to taste it creates maximum satisfaction; so is the virtue of love. A little love displayed that may look ordinary could be the mend of a broken heart or spirit. Most people only appreciate love when it is expressed in a qualitative manner rather than in its quantitative state. They are not ready to know how much you've done but they wait to see that sacrificial deed that creates a long lasting impression.

Love is inestimably expensive, so it must be handled with a heartfelt discretion in view. It flows joyfully retaining no debris on its path, sees no obstacles or the heights as a threat and it's always being transparent. It's truly a meal to savor everyday.

A great spoil - In the account of mount Calvary, it is recorded that the singular act of the Christ's crucifixion brought about the new creation reality, man recognized his inheritance. It is like an individual enjoying the affluence of his wealthy folks who had passed on. He is left to make his decisions and to bear the consequences of all his actions.

A great spoil is the kind of treatment rendered to you regardless of how filthy your life seems to be. It is the kind of love a father shows to his son without considering the gravity of his offense singularly because he came from his loins. If we can properly handle it, we become light to the world through our appreciation.

The Afterglow of joy - Joy is relative. To some people, a million dollar would generate joy for them; to some others, joy comes when they choose to be contented not minding their financial state whatsoever. Joy will not have a lasting excitement if the experience is not founded on true love. You could be joyous over a million dollars but no sooner will you burdened by the numerous ways on how to invest or spend it.

When the afterglow of joy refuses to desert you, you have fulfilled all the laws guiding charity. If you can maintain a joy that seems to never end, it will eventually make who and what is wrong to elude your life.

My home is in your courts - There really is no place like home. It's where you find solace when you need some quietness. It's where you receive mending for your broken heart and where you experience a long lasting love. For most people, they find home when they separate themselves from all activities to reason with themselves and with God.

Some people search the four cardinal points for fulfillment but seldom get it. True fulfillment is based on love and it must be generated from the inside to reflect on the outside. Not all the advice the world has to offer can be compared in appreciation with an iota of the one you realize when you take time out to consult with yourself. Therefore, home is truly in the place of your heart where you find peace.

CHAPTER TWENTY

THE FLAVOUR OF HIS FAVOUR

I can't help but wonder why His favour lavishes upon my soul
When my depth scent with skunk's savour garnished with coal.
I trip over every stone of temptation thrown at my feet
As I climb the mountain of sweat scrambling to sweet.
Every time I lift up my hands to my source, my saviour;
Water cruises down my eyes as I'm enveloped by His favour.
I'm a fool in my paradise, the undeserved being served;
A tool for the flesh, it sometimes looks I'm conserved.

Most times, Nature seems to discriminate and look partial;
Some potential not so essential, some extremely influential,
Still His sweetness is poured on me in stratified quantum.
The Maker's way is one, no one can really fathom;
Not because He created me with a great plan,
Not that I possess all that is sought in a full man
But because He has neither variableness nor shadow of turning
And His Favour eventually locates every man in life's journey.

I can't help but wonder: God's ways are not in the same perspective as men. He always operates in ways that transcends the mere wisdom of man. Man is just one of his creations but he has such likeness for him that one would begin to wonder why. His favour can locate the least expected that didn't even plan for it. God so structured the laws of Nature that it is not how fast or how strong we can nurture our minds to be but being in the right place at the right time we could harness the potentiality of His favour.

I trip over every stone: There is not one man who is righteous; it is by God's divine favour that we all live. As far as you have a heart that beats, you can not escape being tempted. Just as His mercies are new every morning so we are faced with trials everyday and our human weaknesses most times lead us in our own direction. God has made the world this way so that we can appreciate His wisdom and strength in our lives and we can always look up to Him as our Father. We will always face mountains, they will never end but at our command and decision they either give way or become easy for us to climb.

I'm a fool in my own paradise: There is always a way that seems right in every life until we realize the need to refocus and get back on track. If you are consumed with worldly activities then you are living in a fool's paradise. You must know you were created for a reason and if you haven't discovered it, you need to find and pursue it until you achieve it. The hand of time will never turn for you to make up the lost time; you are in the best position right now. Create time, don't wait for tomorrow.

Still the sweet fragrance: The talent some of us exhibit is not something we worked or trained to acquire, it is just a gift by God's divine placement. Do not wish that you were multitalented like some other persons; that one talent you have is just the one you need to expose you to your world. The wisdom of this world demands that if a man fails in his assignment or job description, he is demoted or sacked but God's agenda is far from this. The talent and gifts that He endowed us with are irrevocable; He does not take them back. We have opportunities to return from our failures, utilize the one you have now.

The Maker's way: You can't predict the way God moves or the way He will handle a situation. No one can fathom His plan until they are fully done. Whatever He has created are for His pleasure and they are well created. Once God's pleasures are fulfilled, every other thing falls automatically in place. This is one of His wisdom that many fail to realize as they chase after their ambition. If you strive to fulfill His vision, your ambition will come on a platter of gold.

CHAPTER TWENTY-ONE

LITTLE BEGINNINGS, GREAT ENDS

Little beginnings found salvation delivered on a sheep's bed,
The virgin conception, the wise men are such mysteries unheard.
Great joy was lounging on the world's sad face
Yet it loved the honey of the dark to embrace.

The feet of majesty froze the restless sea
And invalids became valued, barren hearts learnt to conceive.
Miracles were marvelled in the head of vipers,
Still they prepared the venom approved by sinners.

Branches of saviours emerged from the Tree of Life
As ungrateful voices choose to imitate the beehive.
They shot divers arrows in a bid to darken the new morning
To reverse the joyful dance with the music of mourning.

Great ends found men at the peak of resurrection
After the show was completed at Calvary's station.
It was the dawn of a new day, the birth of a new era;
The earth and its inhabitant are upgraded daily forever.

Little beginning found salvation: Most of the Jews were expecting Jesus to be born into a royal family but God chose the family of a carpenter as an instrument to change the design for chosen men in the whole world. You must place value on your little beginning for it has the potentiality to expand. As far as you appreciate it, it has nothing else to do but to grow bigger. His birth in a manger became symbolic to becoming a shepherd.

Great Joy was lounging: It was a demonstration of God's sacrificial love to the world when Jesus was given but many still fail to see it. Most of the great things that happen to us came with the packages looking rough on the exterior; it was the little perseverance we had to uncover its content that paid off. Do not wave off all the ideas that come your way, take time to analyze it and do a proper research because you might be throwing away a great future. It might be time consuming, it may even cost you some money via the consultancy on getting information but if it flies, you'll become a high flyer.

And Invalids became valued: Nobody will associate with you if you don't see anything worthwhile in your life. People will crave after what you portray when they notice you have a selling potentiality. Jesus had something to offer and everywhere he went, people thronged after Him. Nobody wants to hear what you have to say when you are broke. You must look for what would make you become of value and purse it with all you have got. It might drain you for months before you begin to shine.

Branches of Saviours: This is synonymous to a domino effect, it started with Jesus but today we have millions of people like him on the planet. Only a corn seed is required in the planting but what comes out of the harvest is unquantifiable compared to the little grain. It's just one little act of kindness you need to change somebody, such an individual may have awaited that kindness for long. A seed stands alone until it dies in the planting process, grows out as a bud and eventually becomes a tree producing fruits in its due season. We must yearn toward good step not always minding where the credit goes.

Great end found men: The end of every great or small feat justifies the means. It was demeaning and spiteful when Jesus was accused and led to the cross to be crucified. Many thought it was all over, they thought no more miracles would be seen and experienced in Israel but immediately after resurrection, the spread of signs and wonders was like wild fire. It does not only affect the immediate environment but the entire world.

CHAPTER TWENTY-TWO

SEVENTY TIMES SEVEN

Like a sheep gone astray, sometimes I go the wrong way
Seeking the pleasures and ecstasy that turns a man gray.
And I always wonder why God hasn't abandoned me
For in my mirror, an unclean man in actions and words I see.

Though I do the don'ts you restrict me from
But I just see your mercy continually come.
You open my spirit eyes to see better life after Earth,
Took me from the dunghill and the stings of death.

If a thousand years is a day in our Maker's eyes,
I wonder where the gain of greed and grudge lies.
He is gentle as a lamb and terrible as a lion,
Still we frustrate the grace flowing generously from Zion.

Seventy times seven you forgive my lying soul
Each time I step into a mischievous and wrong goal.
I wish the streams gushing from me will satisfy you
As I pour out and render all the gratitude you are due.

Like a sheep gone astray: A shy person who is easily carried away or easily influenced portrays the symbol of a sheep's character. They want to do the things they really want to do but circumstances and especially people keeps luring them towards other ends. If you don't make up your mind to run after your desire, you will end up switching careers, switching goal and at the end wasting precious moments. Keep at the things you really want to do and stay in them, they will surely blossom. Don't be distracted by the things that are 'in vogue'.

Though I do the don't: God's instructions have been laid out to man to follow and make his way glorious but man in his forgetfulness and ignorance always drifts away. God will never force any man to obey His word; He has given man the freedom of choice. Bear in mind that whatever way you choose to live your life, you can't escape the consequence. You must face it whether it is good or bad. If you find yourself far from His way, you still have all it takes to retrace your steps. God does not fail to continually advice you in your steps; it is left for you to take the decision.

If a thousand years is a day: Man lives by the days, nights, seasons, months and years. With God it is from everlasting to everlasting, time is irrelevant with Him. What took you ten years to achieve, may be like a minute in the calendar of God. You may think that it is utterly being delayed but it's in your best interest. You always value anything that took you time to achieve. If we all get things on a platter of gold then it would be like a meal being prepared which you can predict the cooking time and its taste. We place no true value on it, for as soon as we eat it, it is forgotten.

Still we frustrate the grace: The grace of God has been given to us to enable us accomplished everything that we set our heart to do. When we do things on our own and by our strength, we prevent His grace from aiding us in our achievement. Things are easier if we only could recognize that we are nothing but pencils in the hands of God and we are willing to be used to draw, create, and build any line, block or project. Chasing after your own ambition is not a bad idea but what will truly make you an everlasting celebrity is if God's strength is evident in it.

CHAPTER TWENTY-THREE

AN UNMERITED SON

I'm on the loose from the bonds of a strong man
And innumerable messenger rejoiced for me with a band stand.
A banquet was held for the new life residing in me,
Was captive, now honoured with the pastures kings conceive.
Glitters liaised upon the crown that sat on my head,
I saw much undying love for the place my feet threaded;
Still my bowels gyrates to the tone of happy maggots
As the fear of unclean pleasures threatens my blood with clots.

Uneasy tosses replaced the sleep in my cradle
For voluminous seemed the commands on His table.
Decked with ornament of a curious conqueror,
I stepped out of Zion as a new brand of saviour.
I chose the way followed by other spiritual recruits
And found a desert with no oasis but promises of different fruits.
My eyes inquired desperately for a violent impassion
And an unmerited son was my vivid reflection.

I'm on the loose: Every man in the circle of life has his own timing. The time set to have your break differs from that of another person's. There is always a strong man between you and your dreams but God's timing, your faith and the right step to take will see you through and deliver the desire on you laps. Your salvation is so precious to God that when you accepted Jesus and choose to do the right things a big celebration took place in heaven. It's the joy of God to see everyone loosed to serve Him.

Was captive: There is a time in everyone's life when they were utterly confused and they get engaged in any profession that comes their way. This happens when we choose to go our way and depends on our strength rather than God's. God is very patient, He will allow you to expend all your energy if you want to do anything alone, at the point where you are frustrated for seeing little or no effort and you call on Him, He steps in with his own patterns and shows you how easy His grace makes all things possible. His Grace is always available in abundance.

Still my bowel gyrates: The pleasure of sin is for a while but it's funny to always note that soberness comes when the sin has been actually committed. The body is fashioned in a way that it constantly thrives towards the flesh and the onus is laid on you to train it and put it under subjection. The bowel is symbolic to the deep part of our body, the deepest point that craves towards the flesh; we find we do the things that we ought not. Our body always craves for those immoral acts that end up in sin but we always have a chance to flee or resist.

Decked with ornament: Just as a soldier is decorated to exhibit his achievement and status, so a Christian is. We are admonished to gird out waist with truth having put on the breast plate of righteousness and having shod our feet with the preparation of the gospel of peace. Above all, taking the shield of faith which will enable us to quench the fiery dart of the enemy. The helmet of salvation and the sword of the spirit which symbolizes God's word are not to be exempted for they are the greatest of God's desire for us. These are symbols of a Christian spiritual decoration.

And found a desert with no oasis: God wants us all to learn, He will never give us a blessing above our maturity. If we are crawling, He will not give us a blessing that is meant for someone on a flight. He desires all of us to grow to meet up the demands we place on Him. His promises reveal everything we have to know and are entitled to, we have to release His word back to Him to bring them to pass. A godly child is like one in a desert but armed with the water of His word and using it will definitely bring him to enjoy the fruits of God's promises.

CHAPTER TWENTY-FOUR

KEEP HOLDING ON MY SON

My eyes opened to only phase after phase of unyielding toils,
Still I remained loyal to still small purified voice.
Every time I make up my mind to switch destination,
His love spanks me to sharpen my concentration.
And a seal suddenly breaks up pouring out fresh bliss
Making my tempo of confidence step on the increase.
Joy then displays the youthfulness trapped in my frame of clay,
New direction swings in and wipes all my disarray.
My favourite dream begins to echo, 'Keep holding on...
Your place is reserved in the clouds my son'

My eyes opened: Your eyes can be physically and fully opened and you live in total darkness. Your understanding is meant to correct views and perspective; it's what helps you see the little details that you could have normally ignored. You can toil and continue in hardship and mistake it for hard work. Until you discover the right key that will open the door to success, you might just be sweating without seeing any sweet. When your eyes are opened, it is no longer hard work you are operating in but smart work. Everything becomes smooth and easy with proper understanding.

His love spanks me: When you are feeling down and out, you need to sit down and consult with yourself deeply instead running around looking for excitement. Such moments are opportunities for you to sharpen your understanding and think of where you are coming from in comparison to where you are going. This is where the source of your strength lies to spring you from your sitting position with new strength. Quietness is one of the places your strength lies. You need to find that vigour that moves you on.

Making my tempo of confidence: When your confidence is in place, positive answers will emerge from your solace. When you are confident deep down and not in appearance all your quest will end with possible solutions. When your confidence has a high tempo, all your answers will brings and attract to you more answers. Lack of confidence attracts nothing but the fear of failure, past regrets and inferiority complex to the individual. Confidence makes you lively and approachable.

Joy then displays the youthfulness: Joy is the only antidote for sadness. Sadness can make all your physical attribute sag and lose its beautiful outlook. A sad face is never a beautiful face; it is characterized with wrinkles and old age. The youthfulness in you no matter your age will come out when you are constantly joyful. When you are sad, you relegated the full function of your brain, your heart and virtually all your internal organs, when you are filled with joy your blood pumps actively and all your internal organs receive their appropriate dose from my heart. Joy ignites true youthfulness which keeps you away from every sickness and disease.

Favorite dream: Your favourite dream is that number one priority dream that propels you in life. It could be the thought of your new career or your place in ministry. When you think of the fulfillment its accomplishment will bring to your life you are joyful. That dream when kept constant before your eyes has the ability to sustain you regardless of the circumstance you are in. If truly it is ordained and not an imitation, whatever it takes for it to get accomplished will be attracted to you. If your favourite dream is not in-born it could frustrate you, perhaps there's an unrealistic motive behind it.

CHAPTER TWENTY-FIVE

IMMACULATE CONCEPTION

Fresh and clean are my first morning thoughts;
Impeccable of evil insights, thoroughly laundered from spots.
Like a new born from the combs of the womb,
Devoid of airs filtering from the atmosphere's filthy tomb.
Feet like unto fine brass stepped to the door of my heart
And the sound of many waters enticed me to interact.
Page after page of His philanthropy on me began to unveil,
My yacht once more found peaceful waters to sail.
His stab of endless joy murdered misanthrope in my reins;
Fresh blood of vigour flowed through my veins.

Hanging from my freshly painted walls is an orchestral score
Commemorating my overflowing heart and excited core.
The still small voice reminds me to remain a knight
And retrain His love as armour in this very fight.
This had steamed up passion from the depth of my soul
And radiated goodness and mercy at every next pole.
All my bubbles were conserved from any seeming burst,
Now towards eternity I place my new phase of trust.
My once unbecoming being reflects under His construction
And my harbour offloads its treasures of Immaculate Conception.

Like a new born: The experience of the new birth is inexplicable. You have to be born anew to be able to share the feeling. It entails having a total change of heart and renewal of the mind to know what it feels like. The essence of being born anew is to tell others of your experience in Jesus and about Him; this is the reality of salvation. You are saved so you could save others. It's amazing that salvation is not documented as one of the wonders of the world for it indeed makes the one saved a wonder to many. If people can successfully analyze your salvation then it's questionable. When you are born anew, your ways take a whole new turn and your acts amaze everyone around you to God's glory.

Page after page of His Philanthropy: You exist because God has a special plan he needs you to accomplish. You are not alive because you are smart or your looks are super, you are alive because you need to fulfill a purpose in God's exotic plan. God's love cannot be quantified with anything of value on earth; He is the greatest Philanthropist for He is the giver of the air which we freely breathe. You can go on for days without food and water and even with fewer clothes but air is highly essential for human existence. Most essential is His son he sent to die which gave us the privilege to subdue the earth.

Fresh blood of vigour: Everything becomes fresh when you accept Jesus as your personal Lord and Saviour. It is no longer your blood but His, flowing in your veins. A renewed zeal to make everyone around aware of who Jesus is becomes lighted in your heart. It is only the zeal of God that can move you to do the things of God. The intense passion to pursue the things of the kingdom of God is birthed on the same platform.

The still small voice: One of the attributes of the spirit of God is the spirit of meekness. Many people expect that because He is the master of the universe, He has the tendency to announce Himself loudly. God is found in the simplest places. He always uses the base things of the world to confound the wise. The lineage of Jesus had a harlot, an adulterer, a murderer, a carpenter and the likes, not once was it written that there was an important personality in His lineage. Just the way He would never be loud wherever he appears so is His choice of men to be used for His glory.

My once unbecoming being: Everyone that genuinely accepts Jesus as their personal Lord and Saviour had their eyes of understanding enlightened. It is His mercies that locates every human soul and makes us understand what He wants to do in our lives. We were created with gifts and the essence is to use them to affect humanity in His name. If after we are saved our gift benefits us only, then we are under-utilizing it. God knows the frailty of your frame that's why He deposited treasures in you so that when you come to His light you'll have the keys to great rooms in your hands that would present you before men as a wonder.

CHAPTER TWENTY-SIX

SLIDE

Where does the mighty man lie hence?
The mighty man once dwelling in my conscience.
In the past, a warrior, the strong tower was my nest;
But now dancing with the wind and searching for rest.

Where is the unshakeable hope?
From my soul's den it did elope
The confidence of my constant roaring
And persistent longing for the spring of refreshing.

There existed a place where goodness grows,
A vineyard of love unreachable to all foes.
It existed on a hill where I dined with the sun
And made love with Nature in colorful succession.

There is no more laundered linen in my room.
Where can the one mightier than I loom?
My righteousness fails to seduce Him,
For this purpose has been drafted from my scheming.

The mighty man - There is a force higher than your very nature dwelling on your inside, this power can speak to your conscience and give you the free will to choose between good and evil. This is the one reason you are left alone to bear the consequences of your actions whether they are good or bad. There is an inexplicable boldness that a man can possesses when he has communion with this force within him; it's build up an unusual confidence. The kind that at gunpoint he smiles knowing that he has an invincibility that can't be toiled with. You feel it even when you shut your eyes. The minute you stray from this communion, your confidence drops and you become seemingly tossed by every wind that blows you.

The unshakeable hope - There's an unshakeable hope a suckling child has when it has a caring mother always close by. There is an unshakeable hope a man can have when he does everything the right way and he is still faced with problems that seem to defy solutions. This hope is the strong expectation you have, knowing that the abstract will submerge and the miracle will surface. This impetus gives a man the courage to 'constantly roar' that is to remain faithful in the authority delegated to him. There always comes refreshing to your soul at the place where you seclude yourself from the daily beehive of activities and commune with the power within you. This is necessary because there is a tendency to deviate from one's package and plans.

There existed a place: Regret is one of the paramount reasons many people fail to move forward. Whatever happened yesterday is past; tomorrow is loaded with possibility to be beamed with a brighter light. Always remember, God always saves the best for last. Show me the car you've lost in a crash and I'll show you a man who has lost both legs in a similar one. Regrets have nothing to offer other than heartaches and setbacks. You may be enjoying affluence, you may be living in luxury, but have it at the back of your mind that they are temporary. They are as a tent pitched which could be moved anytime. The only permanent thing in life is change.

No more laundered linen in my room: If we justify the wrongs we have done, pride will refuse us to accept our blunders. Avoid nursing the feeling of guilt, it does nothing but add more pains to your heart. Share them with someone to lighten up your spirit. We should show signs of remorse when we err against other people. The virtues of love always look for a clean heart to manifest its acts; love is constantly on the run back and forth the lawns of nature looking for a heart dressed with roses to rest upon. Until we come to a place of reasoning why our source of inspiration and power have left our heart and why we don't feel the spring of refreshing anymore, love cannot erupt. We have to come to ourselves, to reality and consciously choose to do right no matter the case, only then can we slide from our backslidden states into a more fruitful life.

CHAPTER TWENTY-SEVEN

MAMA LIVES ON

I cannot begin to fathom what great loss
That has come and taken from us a colossus.
I cannot begin to unveil her countless attributes
That deserves all reverence and numerous salutes,

Mama though you are gone and we mourn
But your memories shine like the sun.
You occupied your space with large and open arms,
Your life could be written in a thousand psalms.

Mama left this world but lives in our souls,
Every time we touch a life her spirit glows.
An emblem of motherhood with powers of oneness,
She embraced everyone with one and same cheerfulness.

One day we'll definitely see your smiles again
And on that day we shall experience no more pain.
Adieu sweet mother we know you're in a better place,
We shall meet someday when we finish our race.

That deserves all reverence: Honour should be given to whom it is due. If a man deserves respect it should be accorded him especially when he holds a position that manages a lot of people. For if he is a true and genuine individual, your respect for him will bring some benefits to you. When you revere people that are higher in the spiritual hierarchy, you place yourself where the message sent through them has a most positive impact on your life. Spiritual establishment comes via listening, obeying and acting on the words of our spiritual fathers and also appreciating their positions in our lives.

But your memories shine: If you die today and you are not remembered for anything, you have not lived a fulfilled life but merely existed on earth. People who reign as legends long after they passed on are those that affected several lives positively national and international. There is something rich and positive to imbibe from the lives of legends as you model yourself in their lights whether they are either living or dead. Christians holds Christ as their role model and all Christians who want to make the kind of impact He made must fashion their hearts and minds to His.

You occupied your space: Everyone has a space that he or she is destined to occupy in this world. It is in that space that your interest lies and as you function effectively in it you'll realize that you apply little or no effort while deriving maximum pleasure from it. God is not a waster; He created everyone with a mission. No matter how small the impacts of your deeds look, as you keep at it the opportunity to make it a global impact will soon arrive.

An emblem of motherhood: If you don't have a symbol that people can use to identify you with, you are living in isolation. If your representation repel others from you rather than attract, then you need to check your role and your model. People must be able to identify with you with a word or a phrase; it tells how definite your integrity is. Motherhood has an endless trait; a lot of things on earth are represented in the female gender because of the ability that they have to reproduce, be developed and groomed to a higher level. Have a definite symbol and live in it positively.

Adieu sweet mother: The world is a sphere that everyone will one day leave behind to the next stage of existence which is eternity. We all have a great chance to choose what we want to be remembered as and for. 'Many have lived and gone and generations unborn will do same but when they do, it will be note worthy and monumental to know from wherever we are then that we are the manuals the new generation uses as a guide on the path to their destines'.

CHAPTER TWENTY-EIGHT

A THINK ABOUT A GREAT MAN

Like a rolling stone you treaded boldly on time's sands,
Crushing heads of challenges and taking away their stance.
A generational instrument sent to your kindred,
Daring thorny grounds and being in weak heart's stead.
A pope of the populace, an orator of humour;
The life of sacrifice brought the genius seal at your door.

Papa we never did see the potency of your place
Till you translated to eternity leaving this great space.
You passed on not away, touching our souls to the core;
We know one day we shall meet to part no more.
That day Glory will fill this vacuum you left once again
As we all shall gather to never experience any more rain.

Like a rolling stone: They say a rolling stone gathers no moss but God has fashioned some of us to be exactly that way. A rolling stone is sacrificial, having an effect on the lives of everyone and everything it encounters. It crashes every opposition on his path and any challenge that hits him gets broken to pieces. Such attributed to a person is when he does not go after the wealth of the world but true happiness of the people he impacts. Fulfilment is not proportionate to affluence but the gravity of influence you exert to make audience live positively.

A generational instrument: In every generation there are selected individuals that their influence supersedes the affluence of others. They may not necessarily be wealthy and most times they have no specific and major achievement to reckon with in the society, if you check their background you'll find nothing spectacular about them. If you make yourself available in any profession or vocation, you'll end up being a high flyer in it. No one was born a genius without exerting some effort to make things roll in his favour. We are all born with an equal opportunity ahead of us.

A pope of the populace: The common people need a voice that will speak expressly for them; they require the kind of leadership that carries their burden concerning all aspects of their development and growth. You can make yourself a pope of the populace if your life is worthy of emulation. Becoming one everyone looks up to is not an issue that is achievable by oppression but should come naturally from the leader in question. He should be one who can exert a nature influence by his mannerism and personality.

You passed on not away: When someone passes 'away', then they did not make meaning impact on the people around him. If he or she passes 'on' then there has been a translation to a better place of glory, for they left the world leaving good foot prints. When we are in this world and living, we should work hard to empty all that God has deposited in our lives. In the world system, there is retirement but with the spiritual system there is none. Even when the body is weak and needs to retire, the spirit does not. If you have full knowledge of this, you'll be able control the physical aspects of your life from a spiritual bearing.

As we gather: Eternity is sure, our stay in this world is a passing phase. We have all it takes as we are here to become legends, icons and pace setters. No man can achieve anything if he does not have the backing of God. Recognize Him in all you do, recognize what he wants you to do and do it with all your might and recognize His divine power that works in you. There is no one created that doesn't have God's mission as an ordained agenda, discover it for in doing it your ambition is secured.

CHAPTER TWENTY-NINE

THE BULL'S HORN

Everyone said it rarely exists and couldn't be done,
He just grinned and said he would reach the sun.
Amazement entraps me whenever he is men's dialogue,
Revealing his adventures like pages of a selling catalogue.
Decked with the name 'Bull' to spice up his clutch
Gingers the touch that gives his generation a watch.

From distance I admired him refining sweat to hits;
Couldn't blame it on luck but his ability to avoid quits.
He stayed strong on the saddle never sweetening his lime,
Smearing his infection for over all his peers to mime.
I see him keeping his heart good from the bad and the ugly;
And God's endowment will never elude his horns surely.

Everyone said: Just because everyone has the same opinion doesn't make it right. There are many cases where the issues on ground had been concluded from the scientific angle and suddenly the power of imagination steps in to totally turn the situation around. To the one that believes, all things are achievable and there's no feat that can not be accomplished. As far as you can have the guts to conceive it, achieving it is settled.

Amazement entraps: If you refuse to be intimidated no matter what situation you find yourself, you're on the way to becoming an influence in your world. If your life is so full of positive humour that puts a smile on the lives of men, your stories and escapades will not cease from your lips. When your life is an influence everything you do is highly rated and people would want to imitate you. When you are cheerful and energetic, you pull a lot of people closer to you. This is one way of having follower ship in ministry, business and in everyday activities.

Gingers the touch: When you appreciate every positive influence that comes your way, your excitement cannot be contested. When you don't understand the value of a positive influence, you will not receive any stimulation from it. Branding and re-branding create the stimulus to make the value of any individual upgraded, a new style is created and fresh opinions are generated. When you brand yourself below standard, you lose your status and your initial value is depreciated.

Couldn't blame it on luck: When you attribute your results to luck, you indirectly devalue the essence of hard work and determination. What we demand from our destiny is very important because it creates the exact future we desire. When your expectations are based on the efficacy of God's grace, you don't see only your efforts and pressure as what counts but you also see God's strength playing a vital role and the result is always outstanding. No matter how many times you are confronted with the pressures of life, do not quit. When you quit, you reduce the ability to respond to future functional reactions and that could be the best thing that happens to your destiny. When you eliminate the word "quit" from your dictionary, there is no height you cannot attain.

God's endowment: Man is a bunch of talents, a circle of talents that complements each other but he will function effectively in none of them if he does not have a major first. Every individual talent has tentacles and it is best to begin with the one that brings out the greatest amount of energy in you. You are endowed for two major reasons: for God's glorification and for your elevation.

CHAPTER THIRTY

ONION OF A GENIUS

Destiny seemed it wasn't going to survive the night
As he did the necessary, striving in the good fight.
Mean men rated his style among the lowest
But somehow he knew his display was going for the apex.
Fighting lips in browsing the way to greener pastures
With focus on fertility to rebuild his broken structures.
He fell on thorns but spring up smelling of roses,
To buttress the example that no one presses on and loses.

Once tagged with the label 'only believe',
He stirred water to wine for his contemporaries to receive.
Boy of the second will eventually turn men of the hour,
By consistency he propelled one from the floor to the tower.
His inborn gold began to bubble for expression above all;
Never holding back, he broke out like it was a divine call.
He has filled up every space created by his chorus,
As he keeps working the menu, I smell the onion of a genius.

As he did the necessary: There is something particular to do to come out of every problem. There is a destined direction to follow to get to your destination and at the appropriate time. If you do not discover it you'll spend a longer time on the path to your dreams. Everything in the world happens with time and season, you must be sensitive to know when to act and take advantage of the opportunities before you. If you are applying the right techniques and things are going wrong, stick to your act and don't relent because you might just be one inch of perseverance away from your breakout.

Fighting lips in browsing: Sometime people refuse to act in order to avoid failure, they are afraid of what others will say if they fail. If you fail in any pursuit it doesn't matter, what counts is first hand information and experience you learned from it. People have the rights to suggest whatever they think but what counts are the ones you choose to accept and believe. If you believe anything enough and you say it and act it, you'll wake up one day and see yourself having or living in it. Accept only what you have the heart to conceive so you can walk in peace.

With focus on fertility: Be willing to start small as you dream big. Do not lose focus on the final actualization of your dream even if it seems its growth will not finally come to full age. In nursing and cultivation of plants, no matter how much you believe they will grow well; all you need to do to see a robust harvest is to add manure or plant on the right soil. If you need to see a brilliant result, you must apply the right information and method to get beyond your expectation.

Boys of the second: Everyone was created with the potentiality to develop and become what they desire to be. No natural gifts should be looked down upon because all gifts have their timing. Just because the gift you groomed at the early stage is producing fruits do not make some others less important. Some gifts bring us instantly to limelight while others take us there step by step. If you abandon what you have, pursuing someone else's gift because you see them blossoming in it, you have chosen to abandon your timing and delay the path to your destiny. Everything will definitely matter and blossom if we recognize their strength.

His in-born gold: Every man is different in composition; no two people have the same personality, style and attitude. No matter how long you copy the character of someone else, you will always be termed as a protégé in their school of experience even though your success is surmountable. You need to actually find where you belong and settle there to become a trail blazer in your role. If you see the dynamic qualities in others and get carried away beyond comprehension, you are just creating a gulf between you and the in-born gifts that have been deposited in you. 'You are a genius in your own right; you just need to find your place to be prominent in the limelight'.

CHAPTER THIRTY-ONE

TESTIMONIAL

'Fatherly' was the feel as I stepped into his abode,
Ovations and recommendations circling the walls above.
I saw a man, who takes the bull by the horns,
Soars where the Eagles dare and threads on thorns.
Philanthropic trophies twinkled in his meritorious skies,
They bring memories of paths many despised to greater heights,
The air about him spoke goodness even in his silence,
A rare gem he is, dinning exclusively with excellence.

Revered in the temple, a doctor in knowledge.
Still he presses in his populace to point full fledge.
Words of wisdom found their way out of his bowels
Never looking like he would throw in the towels
His life is worthy of emulation while riding to fame,
Submitting not to the passionate heat of life's flame.
Chosen to bring Order to our great Niger's intellect
He is a testimonial of blessing, an inspirational instrument.

Ovations and recommendations: Approval is not achieved on the platform of cordial friendship or brotherhood; it is earned on the tables of diligence. If you are diligent and honest in what you do, everyone would be ready to vouch for you on your integrity. For people to doff their hats because of your works means you have taken a great deal of time and patience to build yourself to that level. When you have approvals from qualitative individuals, you become liable to get referral that ranges from the first to even the seventh level.

Soar where the Eagles dare: The Eagles are known for soaring to great heights. When you go to greater lengths to achieve your dreams, you stretch your limit and strength, thereby building your perseverance. The more your dream is bigger than you, the more your limits are stretched. When an eagle notices its strength to go heights is diminishing, it looks for the highest points of a mountain to shed its feather and recuperate. When it comes out again, its strength is renewed. Allowing your limit to be stretched has its own advantage and will do you the most good.

The air about him spoke: Your most noticeable quality always surround your person wherever you go. When you totally ignore it, you can give a wrong impression about your personality to people. If you carry a good aura everywhere you do your business, there's a huge possibility that you are open to the most chances of getting business approvals. This is the evident reason we like some people regardless of their looks even without having any interaction with them.

Reversed in the temple: Holy men are looked upon as super humans and are regarded as demi-gods by most men. In actual sense, they are ordinary being who decided to mortify the deeds of the flesh and abstain from every activity that will engage their conscience in evil ways. Spiritualism has a law that places the human spirit on the highest platform of meditation: it believes that the human spirit exists independently of the body and its composition. This belief has worked in the practices of great minds, for every one of them was focused on their spirit and it gave their bodies the energy to go after their dreams and pursuit. If you can keep your spirit pure and true, it will attract only things that are of good report to you.

Chosen to bring order: Many are truly called but only few are chosen because the many couldn't hold on to the calling, they failed in strength and pursuit. The few pressed on in the calling no matter the storms and tribulation, they did not only rely on their physical strength but more on the spiritual power within them. If you are very sure you have been chosen for a particular assignment, hold the steering of your destiny with both hands and do not look back or side ways, see only the prize at the end and you'll surely get to the end of the race.

CHAPTER THIRTY-TWO

A JEWEL IN THE SAVANNAH

Affection left the beating organ that spreads life in my within;
For men had made my meditation ruthless and full of sin.
So I embarked on a treasure hunt far away from home,
Striving in the Sahel savannah for acceptance and all alone.
Never did it cross my heart that I'd find home in another heart,
Never did my thought register we could be in a pact.
All of a sudden I found gold dust sprinkled on my faculty;
Glitterings emitted from the pattern I now deployed vividly.
I diffused from a realm of half empty to half full;
It was the contagious effect of my intimacy with a jewel.

The returns of your kind hearted deeds left me fresh and green,
Polishing my texture and wiping away all that was dim.
When I complete my course and I'm drifted to the next phase,
I'll keep your neatly packed lesson in a secured iron case.
They shall be the arrows for my quiver in all my quests,
They shall serve as shield for the beating organ in my chest,
You were a key to an unnoticed door in my life
And a brace in one more ordained and risky dive.
Every thought to this savannah reminds me of the jewel in you;
Blessing the day you were revealed to me will always continue.

Affection left the beating organ - No one becomes suspicious of the activities of another without an ordeal. It is as a result of repeated hurts and pains by one and many that suspicion grows in the heart. Nobody wakes up and becomes a sadist; people around us and circumstances we encounter prompt this action. In the real sense, we are hurt and moved because we accepted the conditions causing these unwanted circumstances. Circumspectly viewing this issue we cannot deny these circumstances are from external forces or rather from without.

Never did my thought register - Coincidences in our lives are just to portray that a force more than what we think is acting on the world. When you can hold a particular thought for a long time it definitely becomes reality but on the other hand, some happenings in our lives were not even registered in our thoughts. This is beyond how long you can nurture a thought or dream, it is beyond your perseverance or staying power, and it is a source of strength that belongs to God, the Master of the universe. He looks out just to see us taking the first step of desiring, nurturing and believing and He steps in.

The returns of your kind hearted deeds - Handling a major need in your life will necessarily have a domino effect. One major need taken care of in your life can eventually wipe away every need. One breakout is all we all truly need. You should strive for that need that will impact lives, for that is one of the quickest ways to be known. If you get a well paying job that pays all the bills, you have automatically handled your personal and family, and that is if your tastes have not increased beyond your income.

When I complete my course - Do not rest on a miracle forever. One of the greatest things that have held men down is the glory of the past they held on to. You must be sensitive to know when to move ahead to the next level and you must move at the right time. You must know when it is time to improvise and upgrade for that is the only way you can remain in business. This happens from time to time or else your affairs will lack lustre. You must devise new ways to keep your relationship blazing with enthusiasm, create a new game, and devise a new trick. This will bring energy to your life and refresh your dreams.

They shall serve as shield - A man is a bundle of the lessons of life he has learnt. Every lesson or experience is meant to increase strength and wisdom. If you keep on going through a particular mistake over and over, it ultimately shows you haven't learnt from it. You can fashion your actions in such a way that you don't go through the same mistake twice, it is not impossible. The reason why we go through experiences is to protect ourselves as we forge on towards our dreams. Many things that happen to us are to prepare us for that great dream. Think of it.

CHAPTER THIRTY-THREE

DELILAH

She professed light appearing very faithful and cool
Not knowing her desires was to make me another fool.
I thought her heart took me as the charm of her dreams
And I simply swallowed her dominance with beams.
I gave her the best my whole life offers
Not minding the cost it incurred from my coffers.

She became vulnerable because she chose to be,
Losing her strength and her believe in me.
It's scary to know what she could be capable of;
One day with me she was on and the next off,
Shelving where our relationship sprang from;
Now I abhor the rhythm of a woman's drum.

I trust her like I did demons,
So good at the game of tears and remorse.
Only to quickly forget the root of her mistakes
And desiring once again the icing on evil cakes.
Now they all seem to me of same specie with different grades;
With a toddler's brain hanging in their expensive braids.

Not knowing her desires: Some ladies don't truly know what they want from a relationship. They want to be with a man for a few things they admire and at the same time they want another for some other things the first man doesn't possess. You can not eat your cake and have it, any pranks you are playing on your relationship will surely find you out. No man or woman is entirely perfect; we must learn to accept people even with their unchangeable flaws.

Not minding the cost: It's only when we believe in something that we give our all. Love makes us give our best, in order words; it brings out the best in us. When you see a man being controlled by a woman, he is just carried away by his love for her but the day he finds out he is being fooled, you will not believe the amount of resistance that same man possesses. A man wants to know that his heart-felt love is not taken for granted and that his efforts are well appreciated.

Now I abhor the rhythm: Every man's abhorrent attitude has resulted from an issue that hurt him deeply. The fact that you were hurt by one person doesn't mean all similar people are the same. We cannot all be of same character because our background varies. If you have been in a relationship where you were hurt, it is not time to put all your hatred on the gender in question. If you can search deeply and accept the blame, you will see where you slipped and allowed yourself to be vulnerable.

So good at the game: To show remorse is good, at least it shows you are truly sorry for the offense you committed but to commit it again offending the same person(s) is a sign of indiscipline. The crocodile's tears of those who hurt us always end up luring us back to their friendship and eventually causing up pains in our heart again. This is very similar when a woman is toying with a man in their relationship and vice versa.

With a toddler's brain: If your man or woman will not outgrow a particular indecent behaviour then he or she must be doing it for fun or on purpose. Even a little child outgrows its baby steps and begins to take firm walk after a period of time. One of the essences of love is to mature the individual and teach him/her how to relate and live with other people. If true love hurts or rebukes you, it is for your own good. If the wounds of a true friend are faithful, your relationship is headed for the top but if it is to spite and despise your gifts and efforts, then it is time to be alone or seek the union where you'll be appreciated for who you are and not what you have to offer.

CHAPTER THIRTY-FOUR

THE DIARY OF A MAD HEART (I)

Hugs and hugs, irresistible hugs;
This feeling began to give my heart real bugs.
It was like streams rushing in innocence
Towards an unknown tidal direction without defense.
Uncontrollable waves of excitement tore my resolve,
Broke my guard and between my strength created a gulf.
One kiss, one more kiss and yet another;
From my religion, my saintly marrow drifted further.

She stared into my eyes for too long
And everything in me started to go wrong.
I reluctantly cuddled her in my arms
And began to recite one of my psalms.
Lost in this fleshly world of fantasy,
I was struggling to wake up and put on reality.
Then light instantly flooded all I knew to be true
And erased the strange feeling that was on cue.

Hugs and hugs, Irresistible hugs - A hug even as simple as it could carry serious emotions. It will do no harm if we don't have preconceived motives. If you had ideas of having a carnal knowledge of someone and you consistently nurtured it, then just a hug could take to unimaginable places. If you know that a particular act will lead you to where you don't wish to go, there's no point nursing its feeling. Stay away from it and let your conscience be free.

Uncontrollable waves of excitement - For excitement to get to an uncontrollable state where it becomes a threat to your resolve, it must have attachments that are either from the seed of love or lust. The ability for you not to be able to control it must have been drawn from stored up emotions that have been waiting for expression. It is better to avoid what you will struggle to control. Excitement in all the forms it generates from is a good force because it can be reformed to become the basis of inspiration you work with. That is one of the absolute ways to control it.

She stared in my eyes - Stares are casual, they could be out of amazement or for the sole purpose of seduction, whichever way they come in, you can tell the intention. There are three possible reasons anyone would stare at you. One could be because they are surprised at your style. Two could be because they simply admire you or what you are doing. The third reason is not that simple, its either they desire to have an intimacy with you or they are staring out of disgust. When you stare at people for too long and they notice, you could make them lose their composition. A few people are masters at the game, you begin it and end up giving up because they are ready to give you overdose of what you started.

I reluctantly cuddled her - It takes time to accept what one is not used to but if you do, you have broken a wall that will also take time to get built. Don't start what you cannot finish; it only displays your instability to stand by your beliefs. There is no virtue in living in the middle of the fence, it's either you are for the right or you are for the left. If you were once living right and you now find yourself on the other side, living against good and fair morals, it takes virtually nothing from you to cross over and begin again.
You may think you will lose a lot but at the end you'll be glad you took that decision.

I was struggling to wake up - This is a very good sign. The difference between where you are and your break out may just be that little struggle. It could be just one sentence, one more push, and one more resistance. You have to do that little extra to cross the bridge, don't just throw in the towel and give up on your strength. A spark of light is capable of chasing away a thousand darkness. We have been fashioned in a way that if we can muster just a little strength, it'll sparks off a full load of energy in us.

CHAPTER THIRTY-FIVE

DIARY OF A MAD HEART II

Love's lowest vehicle takes me down the sinking sands,
With strong wine in my system as my feet drags.
My smiles were stolen and from blissful day devoid;
Sadness beclouded the live style I now employed.
Micro skirts wriggled by to attract my attention,
But my pain was as a hyperactive man threatened by pension.
More micros smoothly glided by
As I blindfolded myself but still seeing through my third eye.

Secular rhythms filled the possessed atmosphere,
Their notes reminded me that I shouldn't be there.
More wine slipped down my alimentary
With my conscience pricking me of what I did purposely.
A man of honour wasn't meant for this kind of trip,
I was allowing my trials to make me slip.
Standing up full of so much grieve,
The brothel I had been sitting I started to leave.

Love lowest vehicle - The lowest form that love can express itself humanly is through lust. Many people have missed the essence of what love should be, even infatuation can innocently pose as genuine love. If you are consumed by your aspirations nothing can distract you no matter the level it comes as. Whatever is of no good virtue will eventually stop you from walking with your head up; it will sink you into unplanned and unwanted situation.

My smiles were stolen - Everyone deserves happiness; it is the conveyor to the best things in life. Sadness has nothing to offer for our time on earth is but for a while, the time we have to display active energy is minute. So be religiously committed to whatever you plan to achieve. It will bring you happiness in the days your strength has grown small. Nothing can take away your happiness if you don't allow it, we have a choice to be in any mood we want to be. People who have mood swings simply chose to have them. The ability to control your attitude lies deep within you.

As I blindfold myself - The physical eye do not see as much as the eye of the mind. The eye of the mind is so powerful that it has the power to refrain you from a particular act. Your mind is what you need to work upon; it is the faculty that gets enlightened. The mind is a very sensitive ground, every action we embark upon first takes place in it before we experience such physically. The mind is where contemplations, decisions, compromise and every failure begins. It must be diligently controlled and guarded.

Secular rhythms - There are a lot of songs that do not belong to any religious categories. They do not edify the mind, motivate the soul or energize the spirit. What we listen to is very important to our happiness because every song comes into our heart and becomes seeds on the ground of the mind. Music is a very powerful tool; it can encourage, soothe and captivate the soul. You can choose to listen to the right kind of song and get yourself uplifted every time. If you decide to listen to music with profane lyrics, before long you'll begin to say, speak and use them in your language.

A man of honour - Honour is a virtue that is not achieved by appointment, it must be earned through diligence and a disciple live style. Honour cannot hide, if a man is due for it, it automatically finds him. There is no short cut to it; it is achieved on a platform that has distinct stratus, each displaying good records over a period of time. Every man has the God given ability to build a brilliant future for himself. It takes a lot of patience but in the end it will crown you with a good name.

CHAPTER THIRTY-SIX

CRUSH

I lived in my heart with the tranquility of sunset,
Everyday was a beat towards the path life was meant.
My coat was tailored and sprinkled with sugar and spice
And it drew the attention of them that were bitter and nice.
The skeletons in my cupboard were exuberant with flesh and life;
I was a friend to the storm; my dues serviced its archive.
No knowledge of tribulation dwelt within me,
All of a sudden I met her and the story changed completely.

It was indeed a wonderful day from to never recover,
She lingered longer than any scent science would discover.
My innermost troubled like a mountain of laxative
And I feared that the emission could be fierce and destructive.
Erratic floods swept me off my formative shores,
All I did became surface without consulting my cores.
She exists in my liquids, solids and in every sphere,
I'm all shivers and praying that this feeling isn't fair.

I'm crushed to the bones and crushed to my marrows,
I'm a remote device that pledged allegiance to her controls.
She had me under her arms like the Spanish guitars
And I respond to the tone played by her fingers.
I want to rebel and leave, I want to succumb and stay;
My coat now drew only the attention of what she had to say.
Temptation and trials have started beckoning to my conscience,
My existence is become like one that lives in absolute pretense.

Everyday was a beat: Learn to take one day at a time and you'll see every problem as a hurdle that only requires jumping over.

The problem with most of us is that we do advance worrying, we worry over our challenges, we worry on the steps we should take to get them solved and we worry about the results of our efforts. Solve the problems that come with each day first and set aside others for a convenient time. You can actually do nothing now about what you need to accomplish next week if you becloud your thoughts with it, it will only blur your vision from seeing the beauties of today.

No knowledge of tribulation: Only babies will not experience tribulation. Every man was born for it, thereby giving him the leverage to know more about his strength and capability. God Himself reminded us that tribulation will come but by His strength we will overcome them. Do not toss aside your troubles and sufferings and pretend they don't exist. If you do, they would wait for you in the later days. Handle them now once and for all so you could continue your life in peace.

She lingered longer: We all had crushes when we were much younger even at older ages. Some of us idolized our school teachers as people we intend to have us husbands or wives despite their ages. This feeling gradually drained with time as we faced reality. When the deep emotional thoughts of someone you cherish or respect filters in, give time before you take a step ahead to check if it will stand the test of time. Many marriages have collapsed because of assumption; two people think they are in love and barely days after knowing each other they sign the marriage pact at the registry, and after few weeks realize it wasn't meant to be. It has caused a lot of divorce in the marriage circle.

Erratic floods swept me: Love can make you break all the principles you have leaned on for years. It can soften a man no matter how hard he proves. One way you can tell you are in love is when the attraction you possess towards the other person has no attachment to any personal interest. When people fall out of love or experience heartbreak, they become hardened, closing the emotional part of their lives. Genuine love is the originality of a crush for it will stand in any weather, forgive any offense and overlook attribute. A crush can be brushed aside by an offense or by changes in looks that do not appeal to the admirer.

I'm a remote device: To love someone is to make a pledge, to stand by them at all times. Some people prefer to dominate when it comes to living with others as one; this is not only unfair but restrictive to the potential of the other person(s) involved. When you control others for too long, you allow them to build up offensive thoughts against you and the day they decide to open up and get back at you, you will not believe the size of grudge that has been stored up in them.

CHAPTER THIRTY-SEVEN

ERECTION

Here it goes, racing down my heart with speed;
Erotic symptoms to which my mind struggled to yield.
There were pictures of how we stepped into the earth;
Stripped of fabrics, blames and even the rebirth.

After all said and the sermon of the beatitudes,
I consequently fell cheaply into you in multiples.
My genius of fertility, the instrument of my flesh;
Rises and falls at that place all timid hearts thresh.

The blood of these unclean thoughts gushes down
Leaving my heart to strengthen my virginity crown
As your beauty roves around my frail estate
Holding me spellbound at all ends like a checkmate.

Since you melted in my liquid world
I'm charred by your chastity and totally gored.
Look at me I stand like the Egyptian pyramids
Erected like a war-front gun in the battle fields.

Erotic symptoms: Lust is inevitable if you cannot control your five senses. Some people think if they don't look at something lustfully they cannot be tempted to fall by it but it's not only the sense of sight can make one prone to wrong doings. If you can control all your senses you can control your life. Those who choose eroticism as an art have decided to allow corruptible seed grow up in the fields of their hearts. On the other hand, you can groom your heart to a point where it repels any seed of discord and corruption on its own accord, meaning that it decides not to move by whatever comes in.

Stripped of fabrics: The label and style of clothing we put on can speak outwardly for our inward personality. The fact that someone always looks very flashy and nice doesn't mean you should or should not accept the fellow. Get to know people up close before you judge or conclude on them. The world has become a stage where many of us are carried away by flamboyancy and sight. We should learn to appreciate the value of the inward personality. You should not be moved by what you see or hear but be moved by your mind's eye and listen to the voice of your heart. The things to which you yield constantly shape your destiny.

My genius of fertility: Majority says that the proof of manhood is the ability to procreate; this is just a surface conclusion. Your manhood or womanhood speaks about your courage and strength, the ability to be able to utilize them in the role of your gender. A man who is consistent artistic or skilled in a role he has chosen and can also function in his marital life as a husband and father displays true manhood. A woman is as symbol of womanhood when she fulfils every vow that constitutes a virtuous woman by taking her entire home as her number one priority.

Holding me at all ends: In the beholder's eyes lies the essence why what is before them is term as beauty. 'Beauty is a spectrum; it means different things to different people'. The experience you feel when you behold a particular view varies to what someone else will. What can hold you spell bound and sweep you off your feet could just be an eye sore to someone else. In all, it is paramount we respect each other's feeling and recognize the fact that our configurations are different. Our various views and opinions are what make life interesting and a mystery which is continually unravelled.

Erected like a war-front gun: A reactive individual is moved by what he sees, hears or feels while the proactive ones do not wait for external forces to motivate them, they go ahead to make things move. Whichever way you have chosen to get things done, be very mindful of timing. Be ever ready to confront your challenges and fears as they come, do not let the genius in you stay cold, react with it. Whatever you are displaying be it manhood or womanhood, recognize that you have more than enough sexual powers that could be converted to become the fuel for fertility in respect of any witty invention.

CHAPTER THIRTY-EIGHT

HERE LIES THE TOMBSTONE

Here lies the once evergreen forest
Where all was full of love and rest.
Our love was the envy of every gene,
She was a blessing to me from heaven.

She missed the master key to the mystery
That a seed was more than one more tree.
She was carried away by glamour,
Easily drowned by unceremonious humour.

The tree we nurtured is cut down,
So many tears and one more frown.
No man can eat his cake and have it,
Running bowels must follow after much sweet.

She kept me as a second option for triple years
And lent the wind all her cautions and cares.
What started on the platter of simplicity
Has explicitly brought me to an unusual fix.

I pray my thoughts won't remember her again
So I could be free to fly above the rain
And tread paths alone with one vision,
No more with any woman's permission.

A woman's heart is truly a deep ocean,
No man can predict the jury of its institution.
She was the last woman I was to trust,
Now my hopes are a valueless as frost.

She baked my heart into glass,
Pampered me as we flew first class
And finally left me in mid-air without parachute;
I'm in pieces, totally paralyzed and mute.

The speed into deadness gave me a total break,
I desire a brand a new energy to awake
So I could refresh from this stale morgue air;
This grave burden is too hard for me to bear.

She was a blessing: Having a good companion is one of the best things that can happen to anyone especially when the companion is of the opposite sex. You are able to share ideologies that are not same with yours. This makes conversation exciting and educative as it is. A blessing empowers you with the divine ability to achieve your set goals. In essence, with a good friend close to you, you are guided in the path to goodness and wealth. If a woman has a good man by her side, success is inevitable and vice versa.

Forgetting that a seed: Do not despise good people because they don't have money. Money can't buy all the good things in life, there are some issues no amount of money can solve but a little advice. The fact that someone is finding things difficult or trying to find his feet on the sands of life doesn't mean the person shouldn't be your friend. Some of us have the habit of keeping away from friends that are not rich because we are scared that they will drain us with requests for help. Everything you have you were freely given, do not hesitate to help a friend truly in distress.

Running bowels: One of the Laws of Nature demands that we reap what we sow. It is an undeniable law that cannot be cheated. A man that purposely takes sugar without control should be ready to cope with running bowels. One that decides to get drunk with alcohol should be ready to face the consequences of regretting later. Once you have eaten your cake, it remain so, if you want your dignity unsoiled then you must not compromise your integrity. One little mistake you make can tarnish your ten acts of integrity.

And lent the wind: The longer relationships are, the more delicate they become. When a relationship is in its early stage, forgiving each other on the grounds of infidelity is easy but for a relationship that has gone on for many years, it poses a big threat. If after knowing each other for so long, a fault such as infidelity is inexcusable, it is a breach of the trust you shared. Double dating is a time waster, it will only end up not bringing things that are pure and straight forward to the individual engaged in it. There are some things in which compromise is not negotiable; a long standing relationship that has built up trust is one of them.

She baked my heart: It is surprising to note that some folks have programmed their heart not to ever fall in love because of heartbreaks of the past. They have chosen not to believe that love exists in the world again. It is only the love of God that can heal such hearts because it will be very difficult to convince them of true love between individuals. Love is the only thing that heals a broken heart so it could learn to trust again, apart from that; they will continually wallow in their emotions and misjudge it.

CHAPTER THIRTY-NINE

SHE DOESN'T

Her smile shone and she twinkled in her spotless gown
While I nodded to cheers from peers like a new celebrity in town.
I sensed envy peering and wishing for our interlocking union
But the choristers' symphony gave no place for evil intention.
From burning strings of wounded violins and a whispering saxophone,
Bliss took charge of the confines of our ceremonial zone.

The silent smiles from mothers suggested lots of positive approval
And the fathers' expressions relayed I was doing the essential.
Locked I was in euphoria of Philo as we stepped up the aisle,
Then my father-in-law entrusted me his gem with a smile.
Very willing my tongue spoke what I instructed it ... 'I do';
I shut my eyes waiting and by a million hours flew.
And her response suddenly hit me like a thunder bolt;
My heart is pierced every time her echo resounds ... 'I don't'.

While I nodded to cheers - A man doing what he has to do is what makes him a man. When you decide on settling down in marriage, know that you have taken a huge decision that should last for a lifetime. Marriage is an honourable institution that should be appreciated. Everyone taking that bold step should be appreciated also, and this is an integral factor that keeps the union together. Everyone likes being cheered; it generates in use the zeal to do more and act responsibly because of the onus on us.

But the choristers' symphony - Music can control the mood of the atmosphere especially when it comes from a group of professional singers. They have the ability of carrying everyone along in one spirit and one mind. You need a celestial mood at all time to achieve your pursuit, whether it is marriage, career, parenting or leadership. When the air is always right around you, there is no place for laxity, wrong opinions and distraction. Music and celebration are inseparable, they keep the mood of the audience in one accord.

Locked I was in euphoria - Love can make everything gloomy around you go unnoticed. You don't want to know any other feeling even if you were putting your heart at risk;; it could just keep you basking in its euphoria. People have become so hurt that they choose to operate in love but with mutual understanding and compromise. It will eventually end up living as strangers or discovering true love along the line. Love in the end is the only virtue that can cover all despite where and how a relationship started.

Very willing my tongue spoke - For the fact that an idea looks so wonderful doesn't mean it will go far. The originator of an idea always has the desire burning in his/her heart. You have to be extremely passionate to pass your idea across to your partner(s) and convince them of its potency. An issue as delicate as marriage needs to be carefully planned from courtship. The fact that your partner calls you every time, have lunch with you everyday and hangs out with you every weekend doesn't mean he/she likes you enough to get married to you. Marriage is an issue to be critically discussed.

My heart is pierced every time: You experience heartaches because you were not vigilant enough. When you are going on with someone you plan to get married to, you must occasionally sit them down when you notice any change in their attitude. Communication should never be compromised for anything at all because the point at which you lose it either out of nonchalance or being too busy, you lose a very vital key. If dragged for too long, you might end up not being able to open that door again.

CHAPTER FORTY

SPRINGS OF A STOLEN SOUL

Afloat in the milky clouds of concurrent beauties,
On fence edges her lovely thoughts gave me duties.
The birds and blue skies were my companion
While the brown earth lures me to a downcast union.
Enticing and new words flowed from my oracle
And her response was re-furbished words so cynical.

A fortune teller wasn't needed to decode the reluctance,
I read what her mind's pen was scribbling at an instance.
If only I could take a fishing trip in the heart of her river,
The reasons for her answer would be lessons to uncover.
My soul is stolen by her charm as it springs like a fountain,
Ready to soar and submerge but it's treated with disdain.

Afloat in the milky clouds: There are two ways love emerges. It can grow gradually when two agree to be together or it can just pop up suddenly from the blues to take over the minds of the ones involved. Whether gradually or instant, once you have intimately opened up to someone, you have chosen to be caught up in the web of love and put them at the top of your priorities. Love can make you live above all the pressures of this world and concern yourself only with the ones you cherish. It can make everything else seem milky or irrelevant.

On fence edges: Trying to understand the things we do for love complicates the issue more and more. Love is inexplicable, be it erotic or platonic. You get to met someone and in a few minutes of conversation, you are heads over heels and you want to spend the rest of your life with them. It is fine if you say there is an irresistible force that flows between the two of you or if you say you feel so much of yourself when you are with him or her but that explanation is not enough. The first thing that must be in place when you are in true love is that you must be able to have self control and be 100% of yourself when you are with the person in question otherwise you'll end up biting your fingers.

Enticing and new words: It's amazing how love can make you develop new vocabularies and mix up words. "Love is like a catalyst that hastens up the reaction in your word bank". Love can inspire you to scribble down words that will startle any reader. The right words can attract and make someone love you for what comes out of you before they meet you in person. The wrong words can repel and make the person you want to attract see a different side of the personality you are not.

If only I could fish: If you get your head cleared and you don't allow your feet to be swept off the floors, then you can read the handwriting on the wall of the one you want to be intimate with. From their behaviour you should tell whether you are compatible or not. You don't need some crystal ball or a fortune teller or even a love calculator to make assumptions for you. If you profess your love to the opposite sex in a bid to start up a healthy relationship, from their consistent reaction and answers you should know where the relationship is headed. The best medium into someone's heart is time, time to study them and learn perseverance as you do.

My soul is stolen: We all at one point or the other have experienced that moment when we are in the presence of the one we have a crush on and our hearts just beats faster than normal. You can be carried away and throw down your guard at this moment and it would just feel so absolute right. No matter how much you feel you are in love, just maintain a focus that it could be a passing phase. Try to control the things you say and the things you do. Be careful not to make promises you can't eventually keep. Give your emotions the space to stand the test of time.

CHAPTER FORTY-ONE

RAINY INSINUATION

Our ethnics were a barricade we easily subdued,
Fantastic winds and colourful rains we refused.
I became a nursing mother to her lingering thoughts,
Her dreams were all over me like gold and silver spots.

Then her dial came through with the voice of a macho,
A masculine bridge which rendered us incommunicado.
And my hours became like a thousands years,
My own prophecy rebelled and turned my fears.

I roamed on the territories of my bed;
With my brain, my heart has chosen to contend.
Our ebullience and resonance have been washed away
And I reside with the residue of floods, stubbles and hay.

Our ethnics: Love from above, defined and ordained, knows neither race nor barrier. It accepts all culture, tribe and does not segregate. Language and religion shouldn't pose a barrier to love but these days people have programmed their minds ahead not to accept anything from anyone of a different language and religion. Even before you appear and say anything, you have been pre-rejected. This is one source where racial discrimination spring from. It is better to be with someone from a different ethnicity and be happy than to be with someone from same as yours and be unhappy.

I became a nursing mother: Nursing the feelings we have towards someone else will definitely bring the expectations of our feelings to pass. We must be careful about the kind of feelings we conceived, it should be curtailed to check if it's detrimental to our well being. If you nurse good thoughts, the fruit of it will end up being good ones. If the thoughts we nurse in our heart be of bad report, then the fruits will be bad ones. Nursing evil thoughts have ended up in making people committing suicide, murder and harbour bitterness. It's healthy to keep your thoughts pure.

A masculine bridge: It feels intimidating when the person you share sincere love with is being appreciated beyond limits by someone of your same sex, it is worse when your person is practically responding to them. It can create a gulf between the two of you if care is not taken. Do not taste what you are not willing to eat, for in tasting it you are gradually lured into the eating. If you are already in a relationship that you believe in, there is no point carrying someone else along in a bid to enjoy the qualities you don't see in your partner. You will soon find out they too lack what your partner possess.

My own prophecy: The words we speak concerning our relationship can go a long way to make or break it. Your relationship becomes what you say of it. If you go on telling your partner that you don't trust him or her or you exhibit a lack of trust, you are putting your partner in a dangerous position of compromise. If you want a lasting relationship, you must appreciate and say to your partner all you want and need to see.

Our ebullience: Do not give any place for your partner to doubt what you feel. Misconception has broken many relationships. Keeping insinuations and refusing to communicate is a crack creator in any relationship. When you share a problem, you are half way down the journey to its solution. It is very easy to love especially when the person in question is pleasing to your sight and it is also easy to hate when you suddenly discover the one you love is not reciprocating or you are being taken for granted.

CHAPTER FORTY-TWO

A PRECIOUS FLOWER

One cool evening as I walked through the garden,
There she was in a corner where she could barely be seen.
A lovely flower that had vitality and virginity
And other virtues that spoke for virtuous quality.

I nurtured all to beautify her facade,
Gave her dignity that would never fade.
It brought out her radiance like a new blade;
As she sprang out so positive in her new upgrade.

I protected her as a warrior would,
Shielded her from challenges that had no good.
She became the toast of substance and caliber,
And we decided to travel down to the altar.

I gave her all my bearings to control,
And all the commands to dole.
Life was sweet with my bed made of roses,
Love was giving me the right beats and doses.

Then I noticed fading on her petal,
Downhill she drove stepping on the pedal.
I had given her total charge of our navigation,
I screamed and the ditch was our final destination.

A Lovely flower: The physical beauty of a woman is timed; everything that makes her womanhood complete and makes a home should come early, it gives her time to pursue other things to complete the status of the home. If she gets married early and delivers her kids at an early age, it is a good plus. "God made the women grow faster than the men at the early stage of puberty so she could meet up early with the demands of womanhood and that's one reason why menopause stops her at a quite early age too while the men go on being sexually active till late in their days."

And she sprang out: The true beauty of a woman lies inward; it is hidden deep beneath her looks. "Men could make women give them the best of cares if only they would acknowledge and appreciate them at all times". The nature of a woman yearn for attention and communication, if you want to see genuine brightness on her face, always apply those two keys. Flatter her once in a while, it will make her feel good and give you the best of her love.

I protected her: Love is protective, do not be surprised if you see someone overreacts in it and become possessive. If you committed a grave sin against someone who has developed true love for you, it doesn't take much from them to forgive and forget. When you are overprotective, you're simply exhibiting insecurity and lack of trust over the person in question. No matter how weak a man is, when he is in love, he generates a super strength to protect his loved one.

And all the commands: One of the ways to check the rating of your love is to check your response to her wishes and direct requests. Love can make you respond to ridiculous requests without you caring about the side effects it could bring. "God's love between human is the only genuine love that exists, it is the only love that cares about the side effects of our ambiguous requests". He looks critically at what will be beneficial to our destiny and blesses us with those things. Many of us have responded to the wishes of our loved ones and ended up biting our fingers. The next time you're faced with a request you can handle, answer it only if it's not detrimental to the future of the one asking.

Downhill she drove: Love is meant to be a thing of mutual understanding and compromise because no two people have the same composition to fully understand anyone. You will be making a big mistake if you give your woman or man full charge of all the responsibility regarding your union because he or she might end up doing what will break the relationship. Love should be monitored, nurtured and controlled by everyone in it with all rights respected regardless of the age.

CHAPTER FORTY-THREE

WAILS OF A SALESMAN

Days counts by with no tangible fruit for my labour,
Futility encircles me as I lay drained in my harbour.
Obstacles flip their wings at my pitiable face,
They jeer at me for the grass I now graze.
My meals discomfort the longings of my hungry gullet;
Moreover, solace drew me to the quietness of a covert.
There I shared ideas with my intimate core,
Conniving with the silent night for an open door.
I sought sleep to awaken from my dreamful realities
Nevertheless, morning gave me stronger beams.

Sunset again called me to the bar with bottles of friendly rum,
A recent confidant seemingly inspiring my laughter in excess quantum.
The magic of the effective tool of persuasion
Has refused my wand of true intent and intention.
Here I wail at every slam on my colorful incentives,
They became my nightmare, void of vivid alternatives.
My nights delayed the entry of another perfect new dawn
As I reminisce on the gruesome lessons I had undergone.
Somehow, it all had turned me a construct in every decision.
Somehow, it all had armed me with a wiser sling in my discretion.

Days Counts by: Every day in the life of a salesman counts because one never can tell which of the days he'd hit a goldmine that will explode his financial status. In his pursuit he must learn to love each day as the only one that exists, this is a most effective tools he must employ if he must retain a positive attitude each day. "The more people he meets, the more he gets closer to a positive response". Every sales representative that works on commission knows the importance of a second, a minute, an hour and a day because he is paid largely from his daily efforts so the time he puts to work must consume every other passion that resides in him.

Every "NO" eventually brings you closer to a "YES". No matter how many 'NOs' you encounter, if you hold on and keep pressing, you will definitely reach your target. How you spend each day will end up showing what the week will become for you and consequently the months and years ahead. There is always something to achieve in each day. Do not allow the chances it contains to pass you by.

Moreover, solace drew me: Direction and discretion builds up when you are left alone to yourself. You are faced with the task of searching deeper into your soul for answers; you don't rely on people's opinion or ideas at such points because you plunge into your subconscious and seek for ways and means out of prevailing predicaments. These are the best times you settle for ways that best work for you. One advantage of this is that, it gives you the edge of doing your own thinking rather than allowing others to think for you. There is more fulfilment in doing your own thinking because more often than not, ideas and strategies from others may not always work for you. As a sales representative, you should after the day's work, take sometime out to review on where you made a slip in the field, what new methods you discovered that works for you and how you could give your prospects a better deal to increase your performance. Brooding on the failures and deals, you couldn't close that day due to inefficiency or interruptions will only hamper and drain the momentum for the next day's work.

Sunset again: What do you do with your after-office hours? What do you do with your breaks - coffee and lunch? How do spend your leisure? We should seek to spend our time productively to make a mark in all seasons. That little idea deliberated on during lunch break could be the break of a new and improved formula. If you are truly a highly productive person, it will always seem that 24 hours is no longer sufficient to work out and execute your plans. There is always something extra to do to brighten the scope of your organization. You should spend your spare times re-strategizing, rearranging, restructuring and rebuilding because at the bat of an eyelid, sunshine becomes sunset and it will all seem like a wasted day.

Here I wail: You will always feel better when you let out the feelings that trouble you, it has the tendency of giving you a lighter heart. The reason we go about with a heavy heart is that we refuse to share our pains and problems with the ones close to our heart for counsel. Certain things you pass through require the advice of your mentor or confidant; a friend you can call at any hour and talk to. “Confession is the one of the key steps to redemption”. It is wisdom to have a confidant to share our burdens with.

Somehow, I had turned: Tough times won’t stay forever, one day they will be like the waters of a flowing river that passes by; you look back after a while and can’t find them no more. If you pick up the paper where you wrote down ten challenges that confronted you three months ago, you will find out that you had either solved or dropped at least 30% of them. Oppositions are meant to build your muscles and change our position. You always become more experienced after every challenge. Never look for shortcuts, take the bull by the horns. You might come out with scars but you will eventually emerge the hero.

CHAPTER FORTY-FOUR

ROTARY RHAPSODY

Together we revolve on the wheels of our destiny,
Sold out to erasing the pity unleashed on humanity.
Goodwill and better friendship hovers in our hives
And we made the honey beneficial to concerned lives.

In our fountain, fellowship binds us in oneness;
On it we build for the visibility of change in its fullness.
Our hand of love stretches out to the needy sect
And the miracle of formation causes their status to erect.

With our tentacles spread to all faces and facets of life,
Countless visions and dreams of the hopeless come alive
Here we are, sowing in the tender garden of nature;
Our cultivation is painting the world a productive picture.

Together We Revolve: Love is the fundamental element for unity, without love people cannot be bonded together. If genuine love is in place, the issue of factions and cliques will not occur when there is a group of people pursuing one course. The destinies of everyone in the world should have a meeting point that is building and impacting humanity, thereby propagating the love of God. If we all cannot do something to change the world before we leave the earth, even though it's a little addition to affect at least a group of people then we just existed.

Sold Out To Erasing The Pity: Your vision must be thematic, if it must have a catch. The minute anyone reads your mission statement, they should instantly know what your drive is. This will give you a particular line of action to be sold out to. Do not be sold out to many things, you will have all your energies discharged into various pursuits and end up not making considerable impact in any of the feats. 'When you sold out you'll definitely get your gold out'. Be sold out to that desire that captivate your heart.

And the miracle of formation: Formation comes as a result of perseverance, willingness and personal effort leading to transformation. Nothing moves if a force is not applied to it. Love can cause the greatest transformation; it can make a stony heart turn tender. If we come together in love with a common desire for formation, we will exceed our desired result and see transformation. If you must see the miracle of transformation reflecting in your life or a course you are part of, you have to follow the laid down principle that brought the transformed life.

With our tentacles spread: Your vision could have many branches and if you are touching most of them, it doesn't mean you are derailing from the original vision. If you can't stand to see the poor being rendered with injustice, then your branches could be: the innocent that don't have money to seek a lawyer's service when they have a case, the prisoner who is wrongly accused and has no money to fight to get him out, and the poor who cannot afford shelter or food and other similar circumstances. The list is endless but you sure have a lot of branches from that one vision.

Our spice is painting: There is a great joy in seeing the result of your good works; it gives you the ability to do more. The world is a global village waiting for you to explore it. You don't necessarily have to travel to some distant land before you can make impact, you can start from your community and watch its effect. If your course is selfless and genuine, you will definitely see the impact from it; your zeal will surely speak out at the appropriate time.

CHAPTER FORTY-FIVE

COLUMNS OF CHARITY

I sought for a land flowing with honey and silence
But all I could find was the thick vegetation of violence.
Thorn of wickedness choked the buoyant growing greens
And my impetus summoned up strength for better origins.

Then I saw a Pebble thrown in this sea of confusion,
Ripples of charity sprouted and spread in a quick succession.
Like David's stone which brought down the wall of Goliath,
The power of Love responded on the charitable path.

The overflow of joy took over the tears of horror,
Frowns transformed themselves to smile on men's mirror.
Then came warmth for everyone in the vicinity,
Every talent found room to exhibit its beauty.

Columns after columns His essence was revealed,
The angel of charity broke the seal that was concealed.
There was sufficient bliss in the air for everyone
And Love stood against odds that made men grief and mourn.

Land flowing with milk and honey: The world is constantly changing on a daily basis; it has never remained static. Violence can't be entirely stopped though controlled. The rate of its increase sometimes keeps you wondering if the world could really become a better place. It is our social responsibility to make it better. If individually we can **act good, think good and see good** in all things, our land will become a place flowing with milk and honey submerging the vegetation of violence. Life is beautiful but the corruption in the minds often strives to choke the beauty that encompasses it. If you can work towards helping others to get what they want with a commitment above self, what you yourself desire will arrive on a platter of gold. The egocentric nature of man and pride are the greatest weeds aggravating humanity's vegetation. If individually we can possess a heart of charity, the world will truly become a better place.

Ripples of charity sprouted: The process of acting good aforementioned, has the sporadic effect of making a situation change from its degrading state. We should individually indulge in at least one good deed everyday. It could be investing in someone's future morally or financially, putting a smile on the face of the less privileged; the widows, the orphans, the fatherless and even the prisoners if need be, or just sharing about the goodness of God with somebody, things may drift much faster than we expect, action must back our words. 'One little deed could give a multitude their feed'. Visibly, David's stone was tiny and it lacked the potency of creating a miracle, yet it brought down Goliath destroying the fears in the hearts of thousands of men. So is a good act, very contagious, it takes no permission from us but keeps spreading joy on the faces of people and causing immense changes wherever it displays.

Every talent found room: School education is just a tip of success's iceberg. It is the training process of enlightenment and exposure to the world of different tongues and tribes. For you to make the impact that will stand the test of time, you have to launch with the supernaturally endowed talents that generates enthusiasm in your heart. Talents are gifts given to us by nature to differentiate us from one another in terms of uniqueness, ability and capability. You never know how far a talent can take you and how much it is worth until you put it to play and exhibit it. Your passions, interests and most of the things that bring out the best in you are preludes to discovering your hidden talents.

Sufficient bliss in the air: This statement takes us back to the third process of seeing good things. The question is, do we truly see any good in how we live our lives and what we do? Do we see good coming out of our relationships? Are we optimistic in our meditation about the varying sequences of life's events?

Good and happiness varies from each individual. For one, it could be when they find a lasting solution to an existing problem that their happiness becomes complete, for another, it could be just finding themselves hale and hearty, and for yet another, it could be the presence of material abundance that promotes bliss in their lives. To be on the extreme, the subject of happiness or bliss cannot be concluding from one perspective, it is relative. If you take a good time out to reminisce, you'll uncover that most of our worries didn't count, they never did occur. Staying happy always keeps the heart in good shape; it makes you lighter and younger. Nobody can make you unhappy without your permission, so staying happy must come from willingness on your own part.

CHAPTER FORTY-SIX

LITTLE FACES, BIG GRACES

Little faces so innocent and tender,
Denied of beauty and genuine agenda.
In droves they search for water and food
To quench their lurid taste for fatherhood.
Their hopes were hung up on galleries
And filling their stomach brought them glories.

Life seemed like a sadist
Who favoured only its loyalist.
It ignores the starvation elongating their necks
Or how they lived in rubbles and wrecks;
With bulging and fearful eyes they stared
There was no secrets but sad tales unshared.

Big graces found innocence's garden and tendered it,
And prepared it to blossom with an ardent variety.
The wonderful colours filled all emptiness
And fatherly bosoms became available to caress.
Then life found the path of caring mothers
Who didn't segregate her children or their fosters.

The fuel of life fed their every desire
And their intellects became ideas to acquire.
Grounds and roofs were under their soaring,
With adopted eagle eyes they became all-knowing.
Away with yesterdays all misery passed
And health is transformed with testimonies dispersed

Little faces so innocent: The best to learn about anything is in its foundational stage, it's also the right period to teach. If a child will do well in life and be filled with love from above, there has to be early mentoring and tutoring. When problems are little, handling them is better. Leaving them to get compounded will demand twice or even multiple efforts of what could have been singularly handled. The best time to bend a tree is when it is young, because when it gets old, you might get yourself bent when trying. You shouldn't despise small beginning because in them are great opportunities to learn everything that will ward off failure.

To quench their lurid taste: Everyone desires to get everything but only the thirsty ones really achieves. It is only thirst that drives a man out in search of water and it is only hunger that can drive a man out in search of food. The stream of unemployment shouldn't drown you but it should be the conveyor that leads you into employing yourself and earning your dictated income. If you deeply desire a dream, all you need to do is launch out towards it and it will draw closer to you.

With bulging and fearful eyes: Don't live your life as a spectator of what is happening in your environment. You can make things happen just as the person you are watching does. The difference between the actor and the spectator is that the spectator has not taken extra time to explore the possible solutions regarding his pressing need. Everyone was not configured to function effectively in the same profession but that profession you find yourself or the one you have chosen via your interest, sit with it and it will drag you to limelight. Don't worry if you failed while trying, everyone that is great has failed at one time or the other but getting up and improvising made the difference.

Big graces found innocence: Check anything or anyone that ended well, you would notice the flow of genuineness from them. Anyone that seems to get everything they desired gets it because of the learning process and time invested to stay focused. When you build on your little beginning, you eventually become a master in your game. The best way to attract the kind of grace that keeps one from a small beginning to a great end is to keep your heart free from anything that is wrong.

Fatherly bosoms: No one can grow without having mentors; no one can excel without having role models. Every religious sect has leaders and models they look up to, likewise businesses and organizations are formed according to the fashion of their existing likes that are succeeding. The Christians model themselves after the life of Jesus Christ and in many cases you can easily tell one is a Christian by mere hearing him speak for few minutes. If you don't have a role model, you will lead an unstable life.

CHAPTER FORTY-SEVEN

THE LEADER'S WAY

The way of love and truth
Is the path that leads to reformation
And the way that bears good fruits.
Indeed I'm leading the way to solution.

The way that benefits all men
Is the path of a good and perfect example
And the way that satisfies the heart and reins.
Indeed to follow it I'm willing and able.

The way that brings men into a pact
Is the path that draws men into fellowship
And the way that seeks to unite all hearts.
Indeed I'm making my excellence run deep.

The way we live in self sacrifice
Is the path that grooms the bud of serenity
And the only way sincere charity recognizes.
Indeed I'm leading with no partiality.

The way of love: If your life is not bearing fruit and you are not seeing any tangible improvement; you are probably devoid of love and you should address it with all tenacity to see results. Love is a reformer, if it has consumed your heart it will evidently show in everything you lay your hands to do. The genuine mutual love between two people of opposite sex is what helps them overcome challenges even as when they eventually tie the knot. Many are afraid of wedlock because they don't know how to face the coming challenges but if there is genuine love, it settles all things.

Indeed I lead: We unconsciously lead others with the way we live our lives especially when we are well respected. You must do everything in moderation because someone might just be looking at you and using you as a blue print for guidance. Leadership is the ability to serve and no one can serve others if he cannot control his affairs, his emotions and manage the same of the people under him. As a leader, you must heed to your subordinate when they call you to order; because there is tendency to get carried away in the midst of activities.

The way that benefits: Leaders must be lovable and they must be able to lead in love and not partiality. When we lead in love, we clear the grounds where oneness will become a watchword among us. When you do the right thing at all times, all your ways and actions will become solution for others. Everyone that looks up to you should get full benefits on building their lives so you must be stripped of self.

The path that draws: If a man is benefiting from you, it wouldn't take long before a lot of people are attracted to you. No matter how you see yourself, there is always someone who admires and earnestly desires that he were in your position. So when you plan to lose your attitude, think of someone who you might have attracted. The path that draws others to you is the path of authenticity. This is where you do all things without pretence, this makes others easily identify our sense of humour and appreciate us for who we really are.

The path that grooms: The pursuit of a true leader cannot be fully achieved when those lead has not found it deem able to exhibit when they learnt. True leadership entails that our actions reflects in the reaction of our followers. We should lead with everything: our lifestyle, our fashion, our mannerisms and our actions. If these qualities have a good starting point in us, it will radiate from the lives of those looking up to us.

CHAPTER FORTY-EIGHT

BRIDGING THE GAP

There is a gap between the continents
In need of our attention and sentiments.
Racial discrimination is burning all our bridges
And making the clink of a new dawn like mere wishes.

Our tears introduce all pains for our good
To make us realize the grounds of gain to brood.
We connect various tongues and tribes
And all races are upgraded with new thrives.

Love in every nation, Love in the whole world;
Love must be written in every sign post and board.
Segregation and racism has no place in us
For together we launch as one spiritual force.

The world will finally see through one light
As we continue in this our might.
If we keep on tracing these disjointed maps,
We shall unconsciously bridge all the gaps.

There is a gap: Betweens nations and tribes of the world exists gaps which only love and unity can fill. Differences in backgrounds, ethnicity and ideology have caused people to operate in cliques and caucuses. Most times these groups are formed with negative intentions which have become responsible for a lot of chaos. Some races believe they are superior to others and go all the way to oppress others, in most cases; these so called superior races even despise their own. Superiority should be an opportunity to show how much you can share.

Racial discrimination: This issue has more to do with our attitude. If you find yourself discriminating then you are probably being affected with a complex problem. Every race has its drive, strength and the pattern to achieve and it shouldn't be a threat to the next. People who discriminate against others are threatened by what they see them display, and because they fail to explore what themselves possess. It will be profitable to learn from all races and know how they get different things accomplished. This can make the world a more developed place.

We connect: Things are done easier when we connect in a network. Unity has its power embedded in the combination of smaller units. The higher and bigger a nation gets, the more it needs to depend on others. No nation can choose to fully isolate itself without seeking the expertise or treaty with others. It will break its resolved at some point. We all need a shoulder to lean on at a time for that is the avenue through which bridges are mended.

For together we launch: When we work together, we achieve much more than expected; when you work alone creative ideas are restricted. Togetherness creates the atmosphere where harmony is birthed and this brings the potentialities of a people to be harnessed in full capacity. There needs to be mutual friendship where the rights of the commonest individual are taken into consideration and the visions of the leader also are to be taken into cognizance. When you decide to launch with the system in oneness, you have added your own power of imagination which tends to bring out a faster reaction.

As we continue: If we want to strive for national peace, we should individually reign over the hurdles in our immediate society. We cannot change the world in a day but we can change our community and make it a model others can copy. If things are working for you, others would want to use your technique. We must see beyond the horizon, the whole world must be seen by every eye as a global village and that is one high way to sentimentally eradicate racial discrimination.

CHAPTER FORTY-NINE

WE ARE

The connection between the needy and needs,
Humanitarian farmers sowing charity seeds,
Health to the deteriorating populace;
We are the smiles on a hopeless face.

Education to the learned,
Sustainable project for the unprotected,
The pull on the string of diverse tongues;
We are the strings that play the everlasting songs.

Examples of merry good hearts,
A show of unity when it interacts,
The images of God;
We are rescue captains on board.

The wings of the amateur,
Coolness to professionally explore,
Like stars in life's skies;
We all are, if we can pay the price.

Humanitarian farmers: The needs of humans are insatiable, they can never be fully met, but if the basic necessities for existence like water, good health and education are achieved, we have hope and a good ground to hold on to as we expect greater things to come. If you provide or sow these amenities to your immediate environment, you are leaving a legacy that would last for a lifetime. Unlike farmers who sow seeds in expectation of a physical harvest, lets us give to charity not to be enriched with personal gains but for change in the places where humanity needs to be restored.

Sustainable projects: There are some things we can do for others that have the ability of not just sustaining them only but also those they are responsible for. If a man comes and tells you he is hungry and you give him a job, you have done this. This will go a long way to solve not only his problem but a series of problems around him. Let us have our eyes on showing this kind of love as much as we can for this is the way our Creator handles similar issues concerning us.

The Images of God: God has made man as a representation of Himself on earth, if we focus on global restoration and development as we work in our individual communities; we are fulfilling His vision for the world. Seeking to satisfy your own personal interest that has no positive effect on the people around you is not an attribute of our Creator. He has created us and given us the ability to create; He made and has given us the ability to individually create our own world.

Rescue Captain: Everyone is a potential leader, even when we follow, we unconsciously lead. We have people who are ardent followers, if they diligently function in their place; they are also role models for others to emulate. When we engage ourselves in various labours of love, we become many things to a lot of people. To the sick we become doctors, to the unlearned we become teachers and even rescue captains to a community rescued from flood. We become the way different sect understands and relate with our Creator.

Like stars: If we live a fulfilled life we are honoured and respected long after we are gone. The stars are more recognized in the nights, they seem to twinkle and assist the moon to brighten the world when it is dark. When we live a life worthy of emulation, we become perfect examples when the world is in search of lasting solutions. There is a price to pay to be great in the little time we have on earth, lets strive to pay it.

CHAPTER FIFTY

JUST LEND A HAND

When you feel it so feeble,
When all before you look impossible;
When the need is for what you didn't plan,
Just lend a hand.

When it's not in your convenience,
When it seems to consume your patience;
When you don't see your deeds as grand,
Just lend a hand.

Your treasure, your talent, your time
Puts nature imbalance on a perfect line.
Just an advice, a page, a sentence
Even a word can make life fluorescence.

When all before you: Every man has his own home zone which he controls, we must individually recognize ours and hold it close to our hearts. The things that look impossible to you are the things that are not within your home zone. When it's in your power to help, do it with all your might. Everyone can render help from their zones no matter how small it is. Do not feel at anytime you have nothing to offer, there is something that you have that nobody else does.

Just lend a hand: Some people have vowed not to help others because they have done so in the past and had their fingers burnt. Lending is living, the more you involve in charitable deeds the more you are sowing profitable seeds. 'A lender is a king, place yourself on the throne'. When lending, it should be done strictly with all discretion even though it's not in your convenience. It is better to render the help that you can do and take your mind off forever than doing and waiting for an immediate reward.

When you don't see your deeds: The reason many of us don't like being contributors is that we don't value the little quota of our effort. Your presence alone can make a big difference. It's not all about money all the time. Your smile could be what another person needs to brighten up his day, just find a way to do the very little you can. A genuine pleasantry or compliment may just be what is needed to feel noticed or wanted.

Your treasure: Show me anyone that has no value and I will show you the one who is ignorant of his precious talent. That gift of yours that you play down upon might just be what your community needs to get upgraded. The realization of your natural endowment will bring your character to a certain maturity where anything you intend to do for another will be like unto doing it for yourself. If we can individually recognize our space and function effectively in it, we would have little or no woes of wants, needs, deprivation and the desperate search for affluence.

Even a word: The world can be likened to an apple that has a rotten part, for the fact that a portion of it is bad; it is termed a rotten apple. No one says an apple is good because a portion is good. The same way, the world is termed hopeless from the view point of a person living in hopelessness and seeing it that way. What you do for one could turn out to what should be done for all. Just a word could pose as the antidote to a poisoned mind ready to perish. Keep lending that hand.

CHAPTER FIFTY-ONE

A KIND OF GOD

We roll on the affectionate circle of goodness,
Challenging facets so life can have presence.
These challenges we grill in our mills of change,
Grading the mountains that made life a rage.

Colourful pages we create,
Mankind's status we elevate.
Mourning is transformed into dancing,
Sighing into inevitable rejoicing.

Miracles are processed in our sphere of influence;
Comfort and bliss sprays from our affluence.
Then the heart of the creator beats in our souls
As the healing of the world constitute our goals.

We roll on: God has programmed the world in such a way that His goodness is meant to follow us as we do well. That means the onus of taking a step before His goodness laces our action falls on us. There is nothing good that can come to a man who decides to remain on the same spot. It's your action that causes a reaction and it's the reaction that motivates you to take more action. We will never wake up one day and find the world void of challenges but our continual circling of good deeds gradually makes it a better place.

These challenges we grill: Problems are better handled and overcame when we see them as challenges meant for our rising. If you cannot climb a mountain because of its magnitude, walk around it, if that seems an impossible task then it's time to face it with heavy machinery to see it become a plain. Mountains indeed can become plains. If we go through life without challenges we will never recognized the role of His faithfulness. Face every challenge that confronts you for therein you acquire more wisdom.

Colourful pages we create: History is accumulation of our daily deeds. Nothing historic happened instantaneously. You can never tell which of your good works will put your footprint on the sands of time for the next generation to follow. One day, today will become the past that will be a prerequisite of your future, make the best of it and take all the advantages it brings. It takes a heart consumed by passion and love to create what will stand the test of time and what will shine in colours.

Miracles are processed: You are created to influence and affect your own world. God created man so he could continue His work of creation, which is why anyone can create his own world and be a top influence in it. We were made in the image and likeness of God, greater than any power that was created; we are the highest power of influence on planet earth. When we nurture our expectations and desires over a period of time, we unconsciously place them in the incubator of life to undergo the process. The outcome of this process is where miracles emerge from. Everything that happens to us is what we have thought about and believed in.

Then the heart of the creator: A computer will give out what you feed into it. It is your input that determines its output but that is not to say it cannot malfunction. Humanity is meant to reflect the life of God and the composition it's created of, but just as a computer contact viruses not put there by its manufacturer so also human are prone to be influenced by external forces. If we can maintain what we have been created to be and refuse to be affected or influenced by outside forces, then the heart of the creator truly beats in us.

CHAPTER FIFTY-TWO

BELIEVE - OUR WINGS

The hands we lend,
The lives we tend
And for humanity we fend
Because believe is our trend.

The societies we secure,
The lives we restore;
With selflessness we concur
Because believe is our core.

The beauty of our work sings,
Recurring smiles it brings.
The bells of happiness thus rings
Because our believe is our wings.

The lives we tend: If you believe the whole world is from one source then it must be registered in your mind that any sacrifice you make for your fellow man is not in vain. When we engage in works of charity, let us have it at the back of our mind that we do it to better ourselves. The world has a spiritual way of turning over our good deeds to us at the appropriate time so lets keep attending to the needs of others in the best way we can.

Because believe is our trend: Our believe can gradually fine tune our thoughts towards a particular direction if we hold on to them. If we have a lot of people looking up to us as we hold on, then we have generated a list of followers. Trends naturally change with time, so we should endeavour to bend and fit in at a positive point so our systems don't become outdated. No matter how rigid a system is, it will naturally get weakened with time.

As far as its strength is not for a positive action, it will surely soften and give way to what you believe in.

The societies we secure: When we love and believe in one another, we secure our race and destinies. When we believe in securing our society we should focus on acting small on our relative capacity while we have the big picture in mind; that is to salvage the whole system. If you don't have enough believe in doing all you can to save the system, quit and save your momentum for something else, for if you perform your labour of love grudgingly, not only will your result be deterred but you have the tendency to pollute the minds of those who are willing to work selflessly.

Because belief is our core: If you see the world as an evil place to detest, you have lost responsibility of your existence. Responsibility on its own comes with a burden to see change and development; we must embrace it so our deeds can outlive us. Every great achievement started from a small believe, either the believe that we can be part of what is to be achieved and participate in it or believing in the positive plans of the leader and allowing them to gradually execute them.

Because our beliefs are our wings: Whatever you believe you can achieve. The sky is too large a space for any flying body to crash into another one. No one would take your place if you are active and not minding the success of others. Everything you do should be to exceed your own result and not to overtake your fellow man. While we experience day time, some other continents experience the night and vice versa, so are the turn of our individual successes.

CHAPTER FIFTY-THREE

THE BUSINESS OF MANKIND

We trade in the business of mankind,
Serving and rendering services of every kind;
Buying into the gloom of the dark and lonely
And paying with the sacrificial cash of charity.

We reject no cases of pits and pity
But handle them with a full heart of sympathy.
Our reward is humanity's love shared
And burdens lightened on every head.

We create a route for all hearts to link
Where hatred and gloom once caused us to sink.
Diligence spreads on all the paths we run
And we adapt gladness when all is well done.

We trade: Life is like a market place, what you bargain for is what you'll get. The returns in your account are determined by the grade of goods you traded on and how you handled your business affair. Everything we do in life systematically revolves on marketing; there is always a giving and receiving, an action and a reaction.

Every act is a transaction sown and the results are inevitable. You cannot expect a large result from a half hearted commitment.

Buying into the gloom: Love creates a meeting point for everyone to trade in life's market. No matter how sophisticated we have become, we can't avoid this point, if we do, then we have chosen to run down the prestige of our celebrated influence. The meeting point love creates attracts all caliber of men and their simplicity has to be displayed on plain tables. When we buy into the ills that have made life a dark and sad place and we diligently seek to upgrade it, we draw ourselves closer to the position where people that matters will come to our terms. Every ill we overcome pulls us closer and opens us up to more challenges and as we continue, we are built us up to face and overcome them.

Our reward: Your life becomes a light to brighten the path of the younger generation when you transact successfully in the market of life; everyone will want to emulate you as a role model. 'Your pattern of solving problems can eventually be a national theory applied to create a change'. Do not be in the party of those who don't want to contribute for fear of being rejected. It is better to be turned down than to be graded as being in the company of the slack.

And burdens lightened: Every solution comes with an aura that lightens our initial burden. The more challenges we overcome the lighter our burdens. Burdens of challenges have an unusual way of not making us see ahead, they make us shortsighted and focus on the problems on ground. When our burdens are lightened or lifted, we are in a better position to think of handling pending issue. If you don't look for a critical way of solving your challenges, the burden it brings will make you go on in circles and get confused. If you can cast your burdens on God, He will sustain you and lead you in the way you should go.

Diligence spreads: When we exhibit diligence in our work we eliminate the rigours of getting stuck. It is not a virtue to struggle with but a lifestyle we should adopt consciously. When we keep on doing things right, everything that is wrong and compromising will eventually lose track of us. Diligence is picking on every little detail and attending to them not minding if they seem less important. You can display love to any person regardless of their race or gender.

CHAPTER FIFTY-FOUR

GOOD SPIRITS

The Spirit of love
Will never give enough.
It bonds us in deep oneness
And keep our hearts in friendliness.

The Spirit of goodwill
Has given us a perfect seal;
It makes us outstanding and transparent
And render our standards worthy of any compliment.

The Spirit of tolerance
Sanctions our lives to benevolence.
To dedicated service we are voluntarily tied
And from the outcomes our joy is derived.

The Spirit of change
We should vow our time and skill to engage
For the betterment of all entities
Through the reforming of our communities.

The Spirit of love: The spirit of love is what makes one looks beyond tribal sentiments, colour, gender and ready to share as far as the subject is a living being. The Spirit of love keeps our heart from pain in the midst of problem, from sorrow in the midst of tribulation and from grief in the midst of sadness. This Spirit is what sustains the earth in orbit and as it constantly rotates and love is shared abroad to everyone. Love is the source of stability, development and productive production.

And keeps our heart: No one becomes friendly without stretching out a hand of friendship. The response to fellowship keeps our heart in friendliness when all our ideas find a meeting point. The evident results are the effective change in the lives of people concerned. Friendliness should never be used as an opportunity to exploit but to network and synergize our ideas because no one can survive as an island. It is paramount that we make new acquaintances as we forge ahead in life, if we don't; very soon we stand alone voiding of fresh ideas, techniques and new trends. We should keep our friendships and partnership oiled by constant display of love.

The Spirit of goodwill: Goodwill cannot be properly defined without the compliment of two, three or more minds involved. Not everyone will lay down his expertise freely; many will request a fee even before an advice. The Spirit of goodwill looks beyond money, time and skill, it focuses on the resultant effect from its good acts. When you imbibe this Spirit, you develop the ability to be honest and open to the next person, you are able to speak up when you are hurt and let all grudges be buried.

The Spirit of tolerance: We all have attitudes that others do not appreciate in us. To live in peace with everyone we must learn to tolerate or absorb certain behavioural attitudes people display. To tolerate is to compromise your principle to have peace in the heart of every body you are dealing with. Check the life of anyone who is tolerant, you will observe a life above self, a life of sacrifice and one who has a deep affection for humanity. The Spirit of tolerance has patience and longsuffering as its virtues, anyone having this spirit must possess the virtues.

The Spirit of change: Change has become so commonly mentioned word that it has lost its genuine flavour to most people. Change is the process of being altered from one state to another. Motion or force results in change, nothing happens if we don't take a step. No one becomes friendly to himself; you must take the step of making friends before being considered one. The Spirit of change is what is responsible for national revolutions, recognizing and adopting it makes our society upgraded.

CHAPTER FIFTY-FIVE

WHITE LONDON

Lovely London fair and white;
How you make my gloom shine so bright,
Cuddling my lungs with motherly fervency.

When I travel in thoughts fair and wide
Searching for motives and priorities to derive.
You bring me back home in urgency.

As I drag you down the filters of fulfillment,
I wear a crown of achievement
Through your soothing potency.

Your hot menthol runs into my soul,
Comfort my spirit and makes me whole.
I throw tributes to your coolness of regency.

How our voyage of romance
Baths me with a chance in your trance
And teaches me to resist complacency.

Lovely London, fair and white: Anything you accord too much admiration to can end up becoming an idol in your life. People all over the world idolize anything in our present generation, ranging from celebrities, cars, a particular brand or label, to animal and even inanimate objects. The God we serve is a jealous one who will not share His glory with any man. He cannot stand to see us place excessive value or respect to what he created rather than He the creator.

Cuddling my lungs: The kinds of actions that give you rest is directly proportional to the kind of personality you have chosen to carry. Different people have their way of soothing their minds. For some it could be watching an old interesting movie, smoking cigarette, taking drugs or taking some alcohol. For others, it could be working in the gym, driving long distance, walking on the beach, walking barefooted on the grass. Whatever gives you rest should result in a good consequence or else may end up affecting your joy with soberness.

I wear a crown: There is something everyone does that gives them so much pleasure and makes them feel eight feet tall. This is human nature for we all manufacture ways in our innards that could complements our gifts; this system stands as a mean of boosting our confidence. You feel a strong sense of achievement when you do the things that are in born and you know they give you confidence. Whatever it is, because it is first hand to you, you believe in it.

Your hot menthol: As much as menthol is used as a preventive measure for cold in some medicine, it becomes supportively harmful in a cigarette. People smoke cigarette with menthol just because of its cooling effect ignoring the fact that nicotine itself is addictive. This is synonymous to saying that there is a way that seems right but the end thereof is destruction. The manufactures of cigarette clearly states that smokers are liable to die young, then why indulge in it and plan ahead to sue the company when you contact cancer from the long standing addiction of its nicotine when you can abstain and live a healthy life.

How our voyage of romance: When we idolize things or people we allow ourselves to be lost in their world. Idolatry is like being in a romance with somebody, you do not care what others think about you and you are ready to suffer unimaginable pain just to please them. Any voyage you begin on your own that does not glorify God and complement His ways can end up getting you in trouble. Search your conscience deeply before you embark on anything or habit and be ready to accept the blame.

CHAPTER FIFTY-SIX

LONDON HERE I AM

I'm back to the irresistible comfort of your bosom;
Into the boat of my former culture, size and form.
It has been a vacation of abstinence from our habit;
The stables of menthol and seeming celestial fire we permit.

Once again you rushed down my jelly drains
Giving fresh caress to all my worries and pains.
In our meditation I found myself on a mast;
I never had enough, always re-firing for it to last.

We were divorced and I went my own way
But my craving has been brought back to stay.
This new voyage systemically pampered my lungs
Taking me places where real addiction longs.

I'm back to the irresistible: Everybody has an addiction either moral or an immoral one. The human cravings are insatiable, we are never satisfied. We wants to do more, say more, work more and achieve more. People easily get addicted to what they take in; it could be food, drinks, movies, cigarette, marijuana, cocaine or any other drug. We are addicted because we fail to hold on to our resolve, the resolve not to be influenced by peer pressure or societal influences. A little trial can take over your entire, refrain from what you do not really want to partake in.

It has been a vacation: Abstinence is a personal decision which requires your own effort and determination. It separates you from a lot of habits, places and eventually your present friends. You must make up your mind from the onset and clearly know what you stand to forgo, this will help you focus on the line parallel to the one you are abstaining from. If you do not clearly check the extent of the outcome of abstinence before embarking on it there is a great tendency it would not last because you will fall into a place of sobriety and feel you are punishing yourself for no just reason.

Giving fresh caress: When you go back to the things you abstained from in a long time, there is a high possibility that you will finally fit them into your values. If you were drinking and you decide to stop, and after sometime you went back to it again. You will find yourself defending the act of alcoholism, stating the relevance of its chemical use and why the body needs it in moderation. When you take a statistic of when you abstained and when you fell back and got involved again, nothing more than a better follower will be spelt all over your face.

I never had enough: This is the true aftermath of addiction, you can never have enough of what you are addicted to and you are pulled every now and then to it to satisfy your fleshly craving. Some people are so down with chocolate and even a particular brand of it that they can make it a meal. If we check the moderation of everything in our lives at every point we will be able to curb our excesses and live as modest as possible.

We were divorced: If you have abstained from a particular thing and you are tempted to go back, think deeply of all the facts that motivated you to refrain, think deeply of the moral capacity you have gained, think deeply of all the wrong association it has separated you from and put it on a scale of preference. Know that going back to that habit put you in a position not just to support it but fully campaign for it. You will find yourself earnestly campaigning for it so as not to loose face from those who once admired you in your abstaining state. Of course you can't hide it for long if you think of it as an option.

CHAPTER FIFTY-SEVEN

EVERYTIME I RETURN TO LONDON

In this land of fantastic fallacy that I'm drifted
To answer a clarion call that gets one addicted.
I overlooked the hot side of the evident mishap
Digesting the desire as you burn towards the green stamp.
And I see the burnt ashes of many failed promises,
The melting of my sacred vows displayed in indices.

Every time I return to London I get false relief;
With you I see an inevitable compulsory death to live.
An evil parading peace but filled with thick dung,
Even the Health Ministry declared we could die young.
I know one day I would abstain to spring up with lilies
If only I could jump from your burning train and dealings.

In this land of fantastic fallacy: Fantasies do not have sound judgments, they are humourous imaginations. A person who knows the detriment of a habit indulged in and still keeps at it is living in denial thereby choosing to exist in a fallacious world. When you are addicted to a particular thing that proves to be stronger than your resolve, you get easily drifted towards all that relate to your addiction. This could be very harmful if your addiction is crucial to the human health.

I overlooked the hot side: The human mentality will forge towards fulfilling its craving no matter what lies before it. This craving for satisfying the desires of the heart is so strong that it sets the nerves on ends and makes the individual have extra energy in store. This extra energy is what gives one the strength to overlook what it will cost to satisfy their desires. Do not overlook the consequences of your action because they will at the end stare up in your face and bring you shame. Analyze critically the detriment of any dicey step you plan to take.

The melting of my sacred vows: Do not make a vow you cannot keep, do not make a promise you cannot fulfill because it shows your incompetence to stand by your words. Your ability to keep your vow takes a whole lot of energy from you, that same energy is what you need to stay off a wrong addiction. If you considered your integrity and fulfiled a promise, you should put it before you in consideration before returning to an addiction.

An evil parading peace: Most of our companies ranging from the pharmaceuticals, tobacco and breweries have all pleasant and attracting way of advertising products that do more harm than good to the body system. They are out to make profit regardless of the health consequence on their immediate consumers. You have all it takes to decide what to eat drink and take as medicine. You shouldn't allow your emotions to be carried away by fanciful advertisements and marketing gimmicks. Your health is the life force of any pursuit.

If only I could jump: You could if you would. You have the ability to achieve anything you truly mean to, it might just take time but you will get them if you hold on. You can stop any addiction that is harmful to your health, your status and your mode of operation. It took three personalities to help me come out of any state I don't like, they are: me, myself and I.

CHAPTER FIFTY-EIGHT

A CHARIOT IN LONDON

I'm carried and briefly honoured on the saddles of nicotine,
Every inhalation keeps a promise of calming the nerves within.
New territories clearly beams on my circumference
Trying to circumcise the image that beclouds my dullness.

The horse takes me through streets of accomplished spaces
As I see my control over people, places and paces.
I smiled fully knowing the multiple implication of my action
But I was more burdened with the clear and present reaction.

This chariot drifted me towards the pull of gravity
Taking me close to the end of its green boundary.
As I surrender my shades of integrity to its tone
Dehydrated I relaxed without a choice of my own.

Every inhalation keeps a promise: Inhalation has to do with what goes into the body. Be careful what you allow into your system because what goes into a man has the tendency to make or break him. What you listen to and accept creates your personality, therefore you must build yourself to that place where you are the one who can influence your words and actions. What you inhale has a promise to deliver to you be it good or bad depending on what you welcome.

New territories clearly beam: You can reach out to all things you can imagine in your mind's eye, if you can keep on the right track. Everyone has new plans, new dreams, new aspirations but not all of us can believe until the end where our dreams finally become reality. One of the easiest things to do is to have a dream, anyone can have, anyone can talk about it but the most difficult thing to do is to persevere and be humble to suffer long in the realization of it. It is better to set goals that you know your capacity can achieve than set unrealistic goals ones which the thought of it alone can destabilize one's moral.

As I see my control: Superiority complex could be very deceptive, it will never lead one in the right way if you display its quality for self interest. Some people think they are better than others with no just basis, they think they do not need to work as hard. Nature is like a computer, it is garbage in, garbage out, it will not give you what has not preconceived either directly by you or on your behalf.

This chariot drifted: If you have made a mistake that overtook you and pulled you to the bottoms of existence; do not give up for there is only one place to look up to. That is upward and forward from where all help comes. God is forever in the business of turning our mistakes to miracles. No matter how far you have drifted away from family and friends, all that is required is just that step towards reconciliation and you'll be surprised to see how things that were paused in your life would gain motion.

In dehydration I related: Do not give any place for complacency when you haven't completed what you've started. Humanity is so choked with decadence that any man who says he has achieved all and gotten to the pinnacle of success is just a beginner. You can never do enough but that quota that you decide to focus on with all your might, ensure the best comes out of it. When you become relaxed your stored up energy is unconsciously dispatched.

CHAPTER FIFTY-NINE

BE MY WIFE

Stylishly she poised, looking like a temptress piece,
Pulling me to touch and caress her texture without ease.
My mind was full of our new found clique,
A union that has apparently brought our link.
I opened the door of her exotic interior
And turned on the key as I listen to her roar.
Her whisper were pleasing to my ears
As I stepped on the pedals and switched on gears.
It was a love affair to cherish,
I would do all to protect her from any ditch.
The means to nurture her wasn't feasible
But I knew deep desires could become visible.
I drove her on lanes and tracks I knew,
We went to all places not a few.
And I came to a conclusion so deep
That this BMW must "Be My Wife" to keep.

Stylishly she poise: Everyone that became a brand name created a style and lived it. If you want people to identify with you, you must have a style. Having a style necessarily does not mean going after someone else's creation that would make one an imitation. It means developing your own content either from a fresh inspiration or from an existing one. You could modify a creation that already exists and end up creating your own and giving you a personality.

Pulling me to touch: The things that we value greatly are things that we deeply appreciate. If attraction will flow from any person or thing, it must be something that we truly love. It could be a house, a car or even a designer label that tickles our fancy so greatly. People create a profession out of what deeply attracts them, others just become so emotional attached that they become freaks to it. What deeply attracts you is a sign of your category of interest if it doesn't fade off after a long time. Some people are star struck or celebrity crazy and go as far as idolizing such people. Whatever it is that attracts you should be used as a pointer to where you are heading.

But I knew deep desires: To achieve anything in life, you must first deeply desire it. The more you desire it, the more it pulls closer to you. The same energy you muster to conceive a desire is what you need to achieve it. Whatever you plan to achieve, if you set a realistic time frame for it and do not compromise on your desire, you'll find yourself coming in contact with everything and everyone that relates to that desire. The bigger the desire, the more time you need to conceive it.

We went to all places: Take what you want to really become to everywhere you go. If possible, rewrite your dreams everyday to keep them alive. There is always a tendency to forget our dreams and go after other things if we don't constantly remind ourselves. When we conceive an idea for a long time without seeing them, if we don't remain steadfast, we could finally lose it but if we can just hold on tenaciously we will get there. If your dreams are getting stale, modify then a bit so they could be pleasing to your mind and with time you'll eventually achieve them.

That this BMW: You must make up your mind on what you want. The human mind is fashioned in a way that it is multi talented; you must find that uncultivated talent and stick to it until it produces. So many people want to become so many things and it doesn't work that way. You end up making so many mistakes doing this. Be known for one dream, be known for one decision, and be known to be the man that kept digging until he struck gold.

CHAPTER SIXTY

THE WAY THE WATERFALL CRIES

In front of me is a waterfall and I stare unblinkingly,
I'm thinking what she tries to say continually.
She goes on and on deeply expressing herself
But her pleas and cries, humanity seems to shelve.
I listen intensively and I hear a song of love,
She says all the love she gives is never enough.

I look consciously into its clear streams
And I see a similitude of my love as it beams.
Every time I fall in love I try deeply to express
But she always sees a fearful reason to regress.
When I try to be normal about my feelings,
She says my emotions do not pass the ceilings.

The waterfall is a man vulnerable like me,
Always trying hard to make her believe and see
That my love is beyond all existing lies
But it's obvious hers will never shut its eyes.
I pray that these tears I and this fall sow non-stop
Will one day make us smile as we harvest its crop.

She goes on and on: Repetition is what makes an advert create an impression on the minds of its audience. The human senses is not normally fashioned to respond to what it sees and hears for the first time but when the message goes on and on, there is a point it gets to and the audience begins to get curious. Repetition breeds curiosity. Most people take Jesus as their saviour out of curiosity and end up loving him deeply for who He truly is. Parents that are forceful with the repeated right words always end up gaining access into the temperament of their kids.

I listen intensively: Listening with your ears and listening with your heart are two different levels entirely. You can be deceived or confused if you listen only with your ears but if you learn to listen intensively with your heart to everything that comes through your ears; you will hardly be found wanton in your decisions. Listen diligently to the tone of the voices you hear every time, you will understand the intention behind it. Not all flatteries are praises, some come with the intention to mock or tease.

I look consciously: Most things that are too pleasant to the eyes are just depicting lies. One of the reasons they say beauty is in the eyes of the beholder is because everyone has different ways of reading what is seen. One person could see a grain of rice and the first thing he reads is food, another can see the same and the first interpretation is carbohydrate. Gold in its original state is not pleasant but after the process it comes out shinning. Make it a religion to look at situations consciously before acting on them; it will save you a lot of mistakes.

Every time I fall in love: The dawning reality that you are in love is the fervency in waiting to express its feeling outwardly. Genuine love can't stay inside; it will desperately seek for ways to positively influence and please the other party. Love is not without jealousy for it can be over protective if not controlled. The fact you are crazy and heads over heels towards someone doesn't mean they have to feel the same way.

The waterfall is a man: Nature is so beautiful and celestial that you can't dispute the fact that the plants, animal even the non-living things like stones, mountain and the sea, don't have individual kingdoms of their own. You can literally see animals understand themselves, the sea trying to say something, the mountain expressing a thought and the clouds blabbing a speech. Everything God has created has a spirit that is why most times we seem to be able to interpret what they are trying to tell us.

CHAPTER SIXTY-ONE

EBONY EYES

Come to think of it, its visual is a meritorious sight,
A peep into the iris unveils more than my teeth can bite.
The system has developed a pitiable and sad face
Where everyone lounges, waiting for redemption on the race.
Love despises every young egghead walking on our streets;
While the society and its norms give us mental splits.
Who will bell the cat, who will cart our wails?
To the higher places where exists luncheons and cocktails.
Tested eyes are sought that habours on passionate heads,
Retina that understands the people's frowns and their dreads.

Your thoughts are coming home, you want to hear me speak;
To share rhythms that'll make your questionable songs click.
Then your mind will receive the revolting revelation
That promises to establish you above the prevailing confusion.
See your future; it's as unimpeachable as clean air,
It has found a reserved seat on history's atmosphere.
Without fear tell all people, Ebony is full of treasures
That is capable of impressing the aura of on and off shores.
Now the sight is transparent, the verdict radiates no lies;
Fasten your seat belts and welcome to Ebony eyes.

A peep into the Iris: If you settle down to analyze your past and the process it took to get you where you were, it will dawn on you that you should never struggle to see the end of every vision you have started. Some of our visions especially the ones to change the face of humanity are implanted in our heart in such a way that we can just do a quarter of it in our whole lifetime. This is the pattern of God's implanted vision because He will do all to make man realize he is not the one who should take the glory. If your vision will end with you, then it was just an ambition, you personally devised and worked it out to make a name in your time.

The society and its norms: We live in a society that fashions a streamed system over time for itself. Leaders build our societies via laws and norms that suit their purpose and political ambition. If a law will expose their unscrupulous activities then it will not be enacted. True leadership entails oneness, the ability to carry everybody along regardless of their tribes and religious sects. Our society will become a better place if we all modify our individual goals and objectives to its fulfilments. The youths should not be ignored because their minds possess more interest and energy for change. When a society is well organized the focus moves from monitoring corruption to fostering development.

Retina that understands: The gap between the leaders and the led is sincere communication in love and honesty. The demand of the led could be magnanimous most times but the meeting point of understanding makes it clear on what should be done. It is better to have a leader who has been through all the society speaks of and about for they will be able to feel the needs of the people and understand their plight. A society that will not listen to the voice of the youths will have its leaders settling trivial issues relating to youth restiveness instead of spending precious time to build their economic stability.

See your future: See exactly how you want your future to be and live in it. The creation of a brighter future starts from mere seeing it. No matter the prevailing situations that surrounds you, don't give up on what you're seeing. If you can hold on in the rains, in the sun and in all the storms; in the nick of time, what you have held on to will emerge like a shinning light. God is the only source of power that can bring your desired future to being; you have to look unto Him every step of the way.

Fasten your seat belts: It is time to sit up right and face reality. Don't see the future as an ambiguous and distant picture. It's time to buckle up and do what you ought to do no matter how long the procedure to see a change in your society. If you change, everyone around you will eventually do and it won't take long before your immediate community feels and lives in it. This is the way to bringing a national revolution. The black continent will see a change only if we cherish what we have and work towards improving it.

CHAPTER SIXTY-TWO

COMPOUND EXPOSURE

Malnutrition grips the necks of happy looking infants
Protrudes their stomachs and bulges their eyes as they chant.
I saw innocent love as they raced around publicizing their private parts,
They seemed not to care that it was meant for only close hearts.
I began thinking how they embraced these predicaments
Laced upon them by lack of civilization and it's under developments.

Ding dong bells dangled from their mother's bare chest
Advertising illiteracy and nonchalance at their best.
Their fathers joyfully send down unrefined alcohol
To torment their livers and render their kidneys dull
In the name of agility and a bid to increase their libido.
For more women and more kids meant bountiful harvest in a row.

I marveled how they lived with no knowledge of their ignorance;
How they cherish their display of fertility and love in defiance.
They gladly celebrated with terms of gross misfortune
And it was clear they had the Maker's plan in misconstrue.
Still I silently admired their simplicity toward nature
As they danced to the tones of poverty and their culture.

Malnutrition grips the necks: The body needs to be fed appropriately both spiritually and physically; it is what you give to it that you see in display. The body has the potentiality to adjust to the kind of meal you give it, do not think you must give it all it craves. It is your mind that actually does those craving and not your body. Your body can adjust to any diet within 72 hours if you are diligent enough so you can decide to be any size and work it out in your diets.

I saw innocent love: Children are the only ones who express the raw forms of sincerity and truthfulness. They care less about the things that trouble men's heart and look towards happiness everyday. If only we can imbibe their attitude, we will see other things and needs gradually fall in place. When a child is angry, happy, and hungry or filled you can genuinely see it and there and then you can address the issue. Adults sow and retain all kind of seeds in their heart which grow unconsciously to become trees difficult to uproot at the latter stage.

Advertising illiteracy and nonchalance: Some people say what you don't know cannot harm but I disagree with the theory. What you don't know can harm you without you knowing the source. So many people have had their lives damaged and attributed the faults to what was far from the actual course. No knowledge of anything is lost, do not be nonchalant about knowing the things that do not give you interest. We are in a better state when we know bits of everything and a lot about our interest.

For more women and more kids: The long standing debate that a man can love two or three women or even more the same is a technical issue. Love comes with reasons and you cannot love two people for the same reasons because everyone has their individual base of attraction. Circumstances can also cause us to love for reasons, the conditions under which we meet, and the conditions of our hearts when we listen can go a long way to create the basis of our love. The only inexplicable love existing without any reason is the eminent love of God.

Still I silently admired: It is amazing when you find certain people live in full blown happiness despite their demented condition. You see the kind of joy that you wish you can express and live with even in your better state. Some people better than you wish they could be like you because they don't know your deep and hidden pains.

Everyone has a level of trouble, the seemingly happy and flashy look may be deceptive, it is best to cherish where you are and think of ways to improve yourself.

CHAPTER SIXTY-THREE

SPEECH

Bind me with fetters,
Lock me up in chains.
Put me in dry deserts,
Where there are no rains.

Pure and loveable words
Spoke man and animals to form;
Sang out trees and birds
From a divine mouth, nature did come.

Keep me in shackles and bonds,
Take all your love for a whole month.
Leave me neither relief nor funds
But don't seal my mouth.

Bind me with fetter: Man was not created to be without problems; in fact they are the true determinant of the size of your strength. 'There is no prize that comes without a price'. A problem free life is a life that will end up without having a history, a life that will end up not making a mark. If you want your name to be on the pages of the book of historic events, then you'd better be ready to face your fears and anything that confronts you. "See every problem as a challenge, see every challenge as an adventure, and see every adventure as a quest that needs to be conquered".

Put me in dry deserts: Nothing was created without eminent potentiality. No place on earth is dry, God never created any dry land. We only have people who chose to make them dry by their actions and statements. What you see is what you get.

See a place as being dry and unproductive and all you get is the unproductive side of that ground. See a place filled with milk and honey and slowly from trickle you'll see a mighty ocean. We all must have a desert experience for therein our knowledge and wisdom is broadened and our ideologies about our existence are structured and corrected.

Spoke man and animals to form: God started creation with words. Every single thing that was created was first spoken. If you have the heart to say it regardless of who is around you, then you just signed up to be a candidate to receive it. What you say is as important as what you conceive. If you keep saying it, you place yourself in a position for people around to motivate you to bring the dream to reality. If no one knows about it, you place yourself where your dream lacks the polish of criticism.

From a divine mouth: Your mouth is divine when you speak the right words out of a right heart. If you can speak out in faith while your heart is loaded with fear; expect nothing. Before speaking out, be sure you have adequately cultivated your heart with the seeds of your expectation. When your heart is in a position to conceive your ideas, speaking it before people you value is like watering it. Their opinions do not really count, what counts is the fact that you are watering the seeds you have sown. Many ideas that become reality don't go untold without having two or three witnesses that can attest that you indeed spoke about it.

But don't seal my mouth: Conceiving the dream is never enough, you should say it, speak it, and shout it. Speak mostly in the presence of those that are there to complement your dreams. They will counsel you in the right direction and contribute with fresh ideas that will get you to your dream faster than usual. You don't have money before you can dream, if you have a viable idea it is equivalent to money with the right person or people listening to you.

CHAPTER SIXTY-FOUR

THREE IN ONE

If I was Aladdin
And I had the magic lamp before my very being.
My three wishes would come in a split second,
For they flow together in my blood as a dearest bond.
My first wish will be to be by your side right now;
My second wish to hold your hands as we walk up and down.
My third to tell the world how much you are valued
And how intense to you my cares are glued.
Every pump of my heart beats your name,
In my veins, arteries and vessels you reign.
But I'm more than Aladdin and my wishes are unlimited
And this strength in me will keep our love undefeated.

If I was Aladdin: You cannot fully express your uniqueness when you desire to be like somebody else. At best you'll always be seen as an ardent follower of that person. Everything you are born to be is exhibited when you are yourself and expressing freely from inwards. You can choose to be more than anyone you deeply admire and respect. Choosing to imitate and idolize anyone regulates you to one point. The very people you plan to imitate noticed, searched and cultivated their gifts.

My three wishes: Do not be in the category of people that wish for the things of life; be in the one that constitutes those who work things out. Everything in life has to be calculated and worked out. Nobody woke up and found what he wished by the bedside, a conscious effort has to be put to play. If you count on wishes, you'll only be disappointed because the confidence you built up in it will only come crashing soon like a pack of cards. You can work out anything you set your heart to do, if it does not work, it will teach you something about the ways of life and build your intelligence. If it works then it builds your confidence.

For they flow together: Almost all men are multi-talented, you find people who can play all musical instruments and can sing and dance, others who can do up to six or seven sporting activities and some are born to be human encyclopedia. The number of talent everyone can exhibit varies but the bottom line is to find a point where all your talents can be relative. They should complement each other; it makes it easy for you to function without derailing from your focus.

Every pump of my heart: There are many things that love can do to you. It can make you anxious for no just cause, it can do make you do everything out of sacrifice and it can also cause you to become unusually excited. When you treasure someone in your heart, the person becomes a consideration in all you do. If the decision you'll take will go contrary to their happiness, you are able to forfeit it without a single struggle. The heart is the first field of play for all the activities of life before they are replayed in the physical.

But I'm more than Aladdin: Man is not limited by nature and the environment he dwells; he is limited by the people he associates with and his ignorance. God has given us the opportunity to express ourselves not minding our physical looks and financial status. No matter where we live in the world, this opportunity is equal. You are more than who you think you are, venture into the things that give you joy and bring out the best in you.

CHAPTER SIXTY-FIVE

MY PEEPING SLEEP

Topsy-turvy showed me the creeps and crawls
As its arrows purposely shot to crack my walls.
My sleep went on vacation leaving me wide open,
Turning and tossing from dusk to dawn and sullen.

I sent my battle of tears and praises to heaven,
Still my reply basket was just full of oblivion.
The Prince kept saying, your weeping is for a night
And the Pauper said, wrap up and take a flight.

Then she came back from her holiday
And I was wishing she had come back to stay.
But she keeps peeping at me from the hinges,
Staying away from me at a thousand inches.

Dear sleep, come to my bosom from the cold current,
Come and have a drink to warm up your gullet.
Lie close to me and pamper my eyes
And I'll never let you go again for so many miles.

My sleep went on vacation: Everyone has moments when sleep eludes them. No matter how cheerful we seem, there are times when it feels like the whole world rests on our shoulders. These periods always look like forever but never really last. Your sleep should not be compromised, for the body and mind needs to rest after being engaged in a lot of activities. When you rest enough, you are in a better shape and angle to aim higher, brighter and better. When you constantly deny yourself rest, your body will eventually force you to take a bed rest via ill health.

I sent a bottle of tears: When you lay on your bed and shed tears of sorrow and regret before going to bed, do not be surprised when your dreams end up in sadness because that's what you sowed in your heart before slept. When you go to bed in laughter and joy, you are bound to wake up on the right side of the bed. If you must cry on your bed before you sleep, it should be tears of joy generated from positive travail over an expectation. If the latter is genuinely done it would make you feel fresh and full of hope before you sleep. There is a set time for everything you desire to achieve, nothing desired is impossible to happen or come to pass. It takes absolute patience and all will materialize.

But she keeps peeping: Prayer is good. It takes every burden from your heart and soul and makes you full of light and freedom. If you become excessively troubled with a situation and you pray over it, it is either the situation is miraculously changed for you or you are changed for it. In anyway it happens you feel better than before. If you can shelve your ego and share your problems and burdens with the one you cherish and care about, the power that resides within and without love works exactly like a prayer. It would consequently set you free.

Dear sleep: Sleep will never be of significance to you if you don't lose it. The day you lay up tossing and turning over a challenge, you will recognize that sleep is a great gift and comfort. Even love cannot make you totally forget your sleep neither infatuation nor lust. They all will recycle over and over in your heart until your mind becomes worked up and weakened and then you will require sleep to be refreshed and revitalized. If you catch sufficient sleep everyday, there is a greater probability that you'll live longer and retain a youthful look than one who gets little sleep because of too much work.

And I'll never let you go again: If you don't temporarily or permanently lose what you have, you won't know the true value. If you set out enough time to think about the things that have happened to you and the people that have come your way, you will find out that they are all sequential to your present state. Value the life you live, the people around you and the gifts inside you. Keep worries far from you, instead think of all the possible solutions to get out of that situation and you'll be living above regrets.

CHAPTER SIXTY-SIX

MEET ME AT THE BAR

Serenity lingers as the money tide stays low,
Twas cold for comfort and all seems relatively slow.
Suddenly an increase in finance and a heavy flow,
Meet me at the bar is all I want to know.

Let wet circles take over every table
And important plans and budget dwindle;
Leave all your sorrows and come in laugher,
Even if the night will be spent in a stinking gutter.

Pay day promoted love and parties at the bars;
Let us get drunk, it's a way to see invisible stars.
My evil desire was a bed of wine to pass the night
Which broke the trances I fall into as a shining knight.

Be drawn from your hatred into my unconscious passion,
Fondle with this ecstasy that goes beyond conclusion.
Whenever you choose a level below your statue of liberty,
Meet me at the bar and I'll introduce you to penury

Serenity lingers: Money is highly essential; it can buy all except happiness. All dreams, projects and aspiration will eventually require it. The lack of it is not evil, it means you have to work smarter and double your efforts to make your accounts stay green. The love of money is the root of all evil. If you allow it to move you it can send you to an early grave but if you maintain your humility when it comes in stacks, it will keep working for you. Many people are only humble when they don't have money in their pockets; that is the only time they can think straight and be themselves.

Meet me at the bar: Going on a spending spree is not a very good way to show you care or that you deeply love someone. The best way to show this is to just be you. Buy only what you truly need or can afford. No amount of money can buy love. If you think love can be quantified with money, think again. If you must buy a very expensive gift to show how much you care, it should be something that will continually appreciate in value. Drunkenness, womanizing and drugs are all forces that could be projected and instituted on the pedals of money. If you can't control yourself when you have millions of it then it is best you strive or work for only the amount you can contain.

Let wet circles take over: Anyone who shares love with you only by means of alcohol does not truly love you but just seeking a compatible drinking partner to be with. If you love someone, you will not give them what is detrimental to their internal organs or total health in general. Most of the ideas shared and ranted about under its influence end up being fantasies and are not implemented. The momentary pleasure derived from alcohol form a base for castles usually built in the air, these dreams diminish as its effect wear off.

Pay day promoted love: People don't celebrate with extravagant parties to make others feel good but to make themselves happy and reignited the important role they pose in the heart of their audience. Money in terms of extravagancy shouldn't be a yardstick for the expression of true companionship. There will come a time when the money wouldn't be so available to throw around and you will find yourself in a place where you can't truly relate with your immediate people. Do not put yourself in a position where you feel you owe everyone that comes around you. You owe no one anything but genuine love.

Be drawn from your hatred: Hatred should not be displayed as an alternative for love; it is the bedrock of malice, bitterness and strife. Learn not to hate anyone for any reason, see their flaws as human weakness which we all have and exhibit differently. If you focus on character deficiency, you will never employ anyone or bring them close to you. And if eventually you do employ, it will take sometime before you lay them off. There is no one that cannot be managed; we all can be managed at different capacities and degrees.

CHAPTER SIXTY-SEVEN

WALLET OF CONSISTENCY

A ginger in my being ascends to update my credo
Which sustains my crispy sheaves at a top crescendo.
I zoom off spending with no reserve like a riot stunt,
The passion ignites my appearance at the boldest font.
My heart repeatedly conquers all quests life could offer
With hope doubling my confidence to be a faithful buffer.
Then my fashion prophesies as grilled sunset in contention
To brighten my camel skin in the image competition.

My big, fat wallet opens its floodgates of nectar
And rippling excitement rushes from my mortal;
Charging the atmosphere and making burdens a feather
So my shoes could be known as the vanguard of leather.
The spreadsheet on me is afflicted with multiple zeros,
With ease I rub shoulders with men highly rated as heroes.
This fetched out the fullness of my consecrated arrogance,
And I keep spending from my dream's wallet without
resistance.

A ginger in my being: You should be observant of those things that make you happy, those chores or passions that keep you burning with excitement; they constitute the key to knowing your direction. The things you have a high desire for points to where you will make a mark in your time. If you haven't discovered what keeps your heart burning, keep busy on the different project until you hit the one you are willing to die for. When you focus on what you are excellent at with all your energy, you will derive satisfaction and magnificent results. If you find yourself good at just a singular talent and you cultivate it with all zeal, it will expose the others and in no time you will find out the full uniqueness of your being.

Then my fashion prophecies: When you are consistent on your art, it increases your zest for living. When your goal makes constant demand on your mental power, you improve on your outcome. Your fashion is a combination of your style and way of life; it emerges from the constant positive or negative choices you have been making over time. If your life is bright, blame it on yourself because you consciously accepted and made most of the decisions that brought you to that place, likewise when it is dull. Nobody can truly influence you without your consent, there is really no one to blame for your present predicament but 'YOU'. Trace back to where you derailed and start working things out again. It's never too late to succeed.

I zoom off: "Enthusiasm is the vehicle that drives us at an abnormal speed but safely to our desired finish". When you are working on a project and you are experiencing a burnout don't relent, take a little time out on some other projects that does exhume your passion, in this way you gather momentum to return to your initial project. Always have some other goals by the side as you work on your major project; they will act as fuel for your passion and aid you in letting off some steam when it seems your enthusiasm is short-lived. This process has no choice than to keep you constantly busy until you release all that burns in your reserve.

I'm spending from my dream's wallet: Consistency on a goal you have a passion for is like a fat wallet you spend from. The more you spend, the more you want to spend. Most people don't derive the pleasure from the money they make but from seeing their dreams come true even though it doesn't pay in millions of dollars. When you keep busy doing what you do, one day you will automatically discover that you are with the keys to the doors that had been locked against you. Many people are blessed with so much money without feeling fulfilled; it could be that they haven't truly discovered the fuel to their exuberance or that they haven't decided to engage in the pull where their strength is tested to know their true capability.

CHAPTER SIXTY-EIGHT

SUPERIORITY

I can hold this complex like a hard piece of rock,
Its fineness circles within me like an active clock.
It's like being pulled by the motion of a royal cart,
Everything trims up to my command and contract.

The confidence I possess bore my imaginary feathers,
To take off and spread with all my momentum gathers.
With cents in my pocket I'm a million dollar,
As I tend my low labour a job with a white collar.

My Pomposity is humble and my pride is gentle,
I twinkle as a new bride who decided to settle.
Super energy is exuberated from my breath,
As I paddle and propel with creation's strength.

Its fineness circles: Some people misrepresent pride as confidence; they are two different attitudes altogether. Pride is an overbearing opinion of one's own qualities while confidence is an accepted opinion of one's own expectation. If you see a man exhibiting pride, it won't be long before his personality crashes and he loses his esteem. There is nothing truly fine about pride, its feeling of pleasure is short lived and the soul it inhibited pays with grief and remorse.

Everything trims up: There are different reasons pride can come into the heart of anyone. When a man stumbles on overnight wealth he is not prepared for, it could cause pride to breed up in his heart. A man that has no money and is proud just overestimates himself. He needs to come to the realization that his talents are meant to be developed to fulfill his purpose in life and not to see himself as a superior being to others. Pride can make you want everyone to do your bidding; it can make you ignorant of the emotions of others. You will see only yourself when you are consumed by the superiority complex.

With cents in my pockets: You do not need physical money in your pocket to be wealthy. If your spirit and soul is in a stable condition, you automatically possess a healthy state of mind and exhibit a wealthy life that only you can truly explain. Do not let your pocket control your happiness for there will always come a time when you will seek after the kind of money you need to complete a project and if you don't eventually get it, your life becomes incomplete. True wealth comes from the discovery of God's purpose for our life and the earnest pursuit of it as we see progress in it.

Super energy is exuberated: This kind of energy comes when our dreams are God-implanted; we know we are in His purpose and it makes us more creative. If you have your hands on a labour that has no percentage of your personal interest in it and you are happy doing it, your energy is doubled. Your enthusiasm grows via positive results from the works of your hands. When you don't see the kind of results you desire, there is tendency of losing interest in putting more effort after a period of time. If you want to see new results devise new applications.

As I paddle and propel: God is the source of all strength and He has created us in His own image and likeness. We have been structured to be just like Him and to do the things He does, therefore you can be what you want to be and do what you earnestly desire no matter the circumstances that is surrounding you. Whatever we need to do the acts of God is in the breath of life He has given us but we need to accept Him wholly and allow Him to lead us and not depend on our superiority or skill. "Allow His leadings to do your bidding".

CHAPTER SIXTY-NINE

GRANDEUR

Splendor splashes over my contour's terrain,
My residence is a diamond mine of inestimable frame.
I'm the sought after, the uncontestable man of the hour;
Camera clicks uncontrollably as I step up every ladder.
Screams circle and pierce the prevailing atmosphere,
Speeches from me fed the famished souls with care.
My ink drags down due to repeated autographs,
I'm an angel sent with the tablet of new paragraphs.

My look imparts hope on the pauper and even the prince.
Widows tend their fatherless from my table of mince.
My crumbs are honored by some as full welfare packages.
The various sizes tend to the needs and wants of all ages.
My eyes kept shut as I fly with the wings of fantasy;
Roving within the realms of recurring unrealistic reality.
I open my eyes and the bells of grandeur kept ringing,
Welcome from the land of dreams, I hear a voice saying.

Splendor splashes over: When we fail to see successes and gains coming from our endeavors, we see only terrible experiences and pains. We must choose to see gains as our relevant result and use them as the bases of our thought for us to maintain a good relationship with everyone. We must see and say the good in people, see the better side of events and everything else in life. This is true optimism. From practical knowledge, it has been discovered that what the mouth constantly say and what the mind's eye constantly see will eventually become. One of the first routes to ply to living in splendor is **see it, act it, and live it** as if it were existing physically. When you are not truly charged up

with succeeding but you keep on doing the right things, you will wake up one day to find yourself successful.
Focusing on success and its elements often lead to even greater success. Being around successful people will end up rubbing off on you even though you don't plan for it. It has a stunning effect on the mind.

I'm the sought - after: To be in high demand can cause you to live a life other than your natural life. You become a role model to many people; they watch your steps and take after you. They dress like you just to identify with you. It's not easy trying to please everybody, trying to be what they really want you to be. In the life of most celebrities, it always seems to be going well with them when deep down they suffer. People fail to recognize their human frame, they expect them not to make any mistake and to be perfect in every way. One little misdemeanor on the part of their character breeds too many controversies.

My look imparts hope: Our carriage has an unconscious way of affecting people. Whether we care or not, it tells a whole lot about whom we tend to be. The way we carry ourselves speaks a lot to people, it goes a long way to determine how people will receive and treat us. If we dress neatly, we will be treated in a neat manner. If we look shabby, we are looked upon to have a shabby mind and we are treated likewise. Our facial expression carries a message across, it has an unusual power especially when we are leading or at the forefront. You can make everyone focusing on us to look like your facial expression. If you frown in front of an audience, it has an impression on their hearts, and they frown at you, likewise when you smile.

My crumbs are honored: What we term as crumbs in our palaces are recognized as pyramids in other people's living room. Place value on what you have and don't look out to others and what they are involved in. It will hurt your heart to envy how others were made.
If wishes were horses, beggar would ride says an old adage. If we take a critical statistic on the effect of natural endowment in human and their effect on humanity, we could discover that

so many people have built and are still building an empire from a similar talent you fail to utilize. We should learn to appreciate what we discover in our lives and use it with all pleasure because whatever we continually appreciate produces value.

Welcome from the land of dreams: Dreaming is inevitable in the life of everyone that desires to reach the top. If you had a dream and did not see it happen, you are better off than someone who did not dream at all. Dream in this context is thinking up an idea or making up of a plan to be achieved. Your dreams always look unusual if your present state is to be taken into consideration, they are always bigger than you are. We are unconsciously armed with what it takes to achieve a dream. if it comes to reality, it's your fault and if it doesn't, it's also yours..

CHAPTER SEVENTY

THE END

We have come to the end of the road,
Here and now everyone must bear their load.
I held you in a secured place in my heart
But right now I open my lid and let you out as we part.
Infatuation beads that hung from my branches
Are fallen and their content spreads like mashes.

We were great friends but not meant for each other
And there was no need for us to go further.
A big burden is released from my shoulders,
You're now free from living within my borders.
It's time for us to individually create our new channels
For the future shows brightness at the end of our tunnels.

Here and now: When you are taking the right decisions concerning a relationship, it will surely bring peace to your heart. If it is for a split then be ready not to go back on your decisions because some of us are better off as friends with no strings attached and no future engagement plans. If it's a wrong decision your peace is instantly taken away and all you feel is guilt. Compatibility in relationship has two phases; you are good as friends and not as a couple or the both parties are better off great as a couple than as friends.

Infatuation beads: One of the best ways to overcome infatuation is to become friends with the person involved. It will help you see that they are not as perfect as you idolize them from a distance. For some, just a mere conversation with the person clears their doubts while for others, it takes longer. Everyone gets infatuated at one time or the other, in this mood you are bound to act and say things which can make you look back later and wonder if it was really you who acted the way you did. Infatuation is like a spell, it can hold one bound and one can break from it easily if enlightened. It becomes wrong when you don't control yourself and take the wrong decisions in it.

We were great friends: Some relationships do not have happy endings, no matter how emotionally attached those involved were. Some of us are able to cope with things of the heart when we were much younger and when we get older we prefer to work with principles. Time helps to create the principles we would eventually live by and help us to carve out the kind of life that we would love to live. Simple relationships with many promises at the beginning could end up with complications along the way.

A big burden: You could be in a relationship and everything just seem so right to you but everyone who looks at you sees so many wrongs. This is because love has the strong potential to becloud your sense of judgment. If you think you cannot forgo a relationship that places a heavy burden on you just because you are afraid of finding another one, think again. The best is always yet to come; you are yet to meet that individual whose attitude and love towards you will blow your mind. It is better to live free of any burden than to allow it becloud other wonderful things to come your way.

For the future: You are better apart as friends than divorced as a married couple. Marriage should not be rushed into; there are so many wonderful things to explore in life. "Marriage is one great institution when you are enrolled in it, you never stop taking up new courses and examinations and you never graduate from it". If the man would allow the woman to be a career woman, then he'd better be ready to cater for the affairs of the home while she's away and vice versa. There is a brighter future when two decide to live as one because the older you become, the more you need to depend on one another.

EXTRA CHAPTER

HOLY SPIRIT, I DECLARE MY LOVE

You've given us your love
Your everlasting peace and joy
Lord we come before your throne
To seek you alone
We can sense your holy presence
And the warmth of your embrace
There's no way that we can repay
Than to acknowledge you in our ways

Chorus: Holy Spirit I declare my love for you
You are the only one that is true
Holy Spirit I declare my love for you
I love you, I adore you and I really do } 2 xs

You've given me new life
And all there is to survive
Lord I give you all the glory
You've change my story
Inside I feel so much joy
For giving me all to enjoy
There's no way that we can repay
Than to acknowledge you in our ways